Lifeonomics™

BREAKING FREE OF WORRY AND REGRET

Robert J. Holdford

Lifeonomics: Breaking Free of Worry and Regret by Robert J. Holdford

Library of Congress Number: 2025918728

ISBN: 978-1-959009-27-6 (eBook)
ISBN: 978-1-959009-28-3 (Paperback)
ISBN: 978-1-959009-29-0 (Hardcover)

Published 2026 in the United States by Create a New Life Publishing, Little Rock, First Edition Published 2009

TABLE OF CONTENTS

INTRODUCTION

*What would you do differently if you weren't worried
that you would regret the decision?*

Rick and Jo Anne had just met with us a few weeks before, so when I saw their names on my calendar, I wondered why they had come in so soon. Very happily married, they were about to celebrate their 30th wedding anniversary. I hoped they were planning a dream vacation or some other romantic experience and looking to draw funds from one of their accounts. As I reviewed their file to prepare for the appointment, I was proud of our financial planning work together. At 52 years old, they were well on their way to an early retirement. Their son, Kevin, was now out of college, so their finances, as well as life in general, were expected to improve. Rick was very clear about what we define as Truly Important to him. His faith in God and protecting and providing for his family topped the list.

Rick showed up to the appointment wearing a baseball cap, something I had never seen him wear before. As he shook my hand, I knew something was wrong. His usual energy and enthusiasm were gone, replaced by something more uncertain. As a wealth advisor, I have developed excellent instincts telling me when something isn't right, and they were buzzing now. The three of us sat in my office and suffered through one of those awkward moments where no one knew quite what to say. It was like a moment from a courtroom drama where the jury is about to read the verdict, and everything hangs in the balance.

Rick broke the tension. With incredible grace, he reached up, pulled the ball cap off his head and leaned forward. What was left of his light red hair fell forward in a long, untrained comb-over, revealing a nine-inch gash held snugly together by several metal staples. Speaking slowly and calmly, he told me the terrible story in a few words. His doctors had removed a malignant tumor from his brain, but the cancer that caused it had already spread into his lungs. He had just been informed that he had about six months to live. He leaned back, throwing his comb-over in place just before the cap came down. "There was not even a single symptom," he said. "They found it during a routine physical."

In a moment of clarity, I realized exactly why they had come to see me. They wanted me to tell them that no matter what happened, *everything would be all right financially.* Although Jo Anne never stated it, she clearly wanted an answer to one question: "Are we going to be able to drop everything so we can focus on keeping Rick alive?" What was most important to Rick, however, was another question: "Is the plan we put together really going to take care of my wife and son if I don't make it through this?"

Feeling...Lucky?

I bowed my head and spent a few minutes reviewing Rick and Jo Anne's entire wealth plan, double-checking to make sure my emotions were not affecting my evaluation. The room was completely silent; I could hear the clock ticking and maybe my watch as well. But as the shock of Rick's illness wore off, I reminded myself that we had planned for this possibility. His disability insurance was in force and up to date. A few short years ago, we increased his life insurance. We had recently rolled most of his life savings out of a retirement plan, in which more than 40% was invested in a single tech stock, and into a well-balanced, highly diversified portfolio. Other than a couple of minor yet important legal documents they had yet to draw up, one thing was clear:

They were going to be able to put all their energy
into defeating cancer.

Relief flowed through my body, easing the way I sat in my chair. First, I reminded them that we had considered scenarios like this in their financial plan. They had very little to worry about in that area of their lives. I saw them both breathe easier. Then I shared with them the story about my cousin, who discovered that she had a terminal illness and went on a cross-country quest to right all her wrongs and restore her integrity in a last-minute but successful effort to bring peace and meaning to her life. Rick's reply changed my life forever.

He said, "Well, I guess that's the best part about the way we have lived our lives. We don't have to travel anywhere or do anything. All my wrongs have been made right a long time ago. All of the people that I love already know how I feel. I have spent 30 years with the woman of my dreams. The only debt that I have is to my God, and a dear friend of mine paid it for me a couple of thousand years ago on a cross. To be completely honest, right now, we are feeling pretty doggone lucky."

I was staggered. I thought, "How could he not be worried? How could he have no regrets?" Here was a man in his prime, about to move toward retirement with the woman he loved, who had built a proud and successful life, only to have it all cruelly stolen away by an unexpected diagnosis that left him just months to live. How could he be at peace with this? I was so shaken that I almost asked the question out loud. I'm still not sure how I managed to hold back tears. But my entire "life perspective" had already begun to shift irreversibly.

Breaking Free from Worry and Regret

Rick was far from giving up the battle against his cancer, but I knew that if he was ultimately facing an opponent he could not defeat, he had lived a life that many people only dream of, a life of faith, love, meaning and purpose. Imagine standing at the beginning of the end of your life and looking back without a single worry or regret. This man knew what was Truly Important to him—and the people who were Truly Important to him. He had really lived his life; life had not lived him. That moment reminded me that I was privileged to have known and worked with him.

Most importantly, I knew at that moment that if Rick could live a life of honor, free of worry and regret, even when faced with a deadly disease, so could I. And maybe I could help others do the same. That moment of harsh truth and what I believe is divinely inspired wisdom have culminated in this book.

Rick lost his battle with cancer some seven months later, but before that happened, he shocked his doctors (but no one else who knew him) on more than one occasion by smiling and getting up and walking out of a hospital room that they were sure he would never leave. Before he left us, I was among countless friends, relatives and co-workers who were touched and inspired by his grace and dignity during his last few months on this earth. Because of his planning, his wife and son have been able to dedicate the rest of their lives to honoring his legacy and teaching the lesson that Rick lived in his final months: *It is possible to live a life free of worry and regret.*

Living in the Now

The aftermath of Rick's stunning news was not the first time I had thought about writing a book like this. I've spent over 35 years as a wealth advisor, coaching people in preparing for and living their lives. I had been thinking about writing a book for several years before Rick's story caused me to finally hit the keyboard. Why? Over the years, I have seen hundreds of clients and thousands of others at workshops and seminars who seemed to be consuming their precious lives with worry, regret, or both. I believe it's an epidemic, especially in the United States, where we seemingly worry about everything. We are one of the most anxiety-plagued countries on earth. As we accumulate greater material wealth, we seem to have even more fear. At this writing, we, as a nation, are coping with inflation, which the majority of Americans consider a big problem, according to Pew Research[1], and we seem more politically divided than at any other time in recent memory.

There is undoubtedly reason for *realistic* concern. However, even when times are great and we're flush, we seem to find reasons to fret over things or to look back and beat ourselves up. Forget baseball; worry is a national pastime.

Worry is the habit of projecting irrational fears into the future, while regret is the habit of punishing ourselves for past mistakes. Both are irrational and destructive. They are habits and choices that rob us of our lives more than almost anything else we do. There's nothing wrong with a little of either one, but when we're *living* in the past or the future, we are most certainly *not* living in the present. Both can take us out of the process and joy of living our lives, which is happening moment by moment.

Worry and regret are the evil twins that can warp and corrode our lives by making us spend much of our time fearing what might happen tomorrow or feeling bad about what happened yesterday. Now, *that's* suffering. Much of the unhappiness and suffering in life occurs not in the present moment but in anticipation or memory. Worry and regret are like diseases that infect people with the compulsion to dwell on what might happen or what has already happened.

---

[1] *"A Staggering 63% of Americans Think Inflation Is a Big Problem—Here Are 3 Simple Strategies for Fighting Inflation,"* MSN Money, *accessed May 28, 2025, https://www. msn.com/en-us/money/personalfinance/a-staggering-63-of-americans-think-inflation- is-a-big-problem-here-are-3-simple-strategies-for-fighting-inflation/ar-AA1DIxOA*

Worry and regret are habitual, obsessive patterns of thought. The body's responses to thoughts are emotions, according to the spiritual teacher and author Eckhart Tolle. For instance, our emotional response to worry is fear, and to regret is guilt. We also have a physical response to our thoughts. Because our bodies can't distinguish between a real experience and the thought of one, we not only generate unnecessary and uncomfortable emotions through worry and regret but also subject our bodies to unnecessary stress as we react to the fear generated by the obsessive thought.[2]

Our fight-or-flight programming kicks into high gear. Our endorphins race, adrenaline increases, and muscles tense, preparing us to spring into action. These physical responses seem to validate the worry, fooling us into believing that *something is wrong* or *that our intuition is telling us we are justified in our worry.* This is a perfect example of the tail wagging the dog. We think we are following our feelings, but our feelings are following our thoughts, which we have habitually allowed to run amok like a spoiled child in a nice restaurant. Our feelings feed more obsessive thinking, and we create a vicious cycle that's very hard to break.

An Exponential Change

What might happen if we *could* learn not to worry and regret so much? It could bring about an exponential change in happiness, peace, and the reduction of stress, giving us back a large percentage of the time we lose to those habits of thought. If we lived more in the present moment, we would be better able to enjoy the things that only have meaning right now: a baby's cooing, art, the feeling of being alone in nature, exhilarating acts like snow skiing or paddling down rapids, making love. There is very little fear or suffering in the present moment. Worrying about test results,

---

[2] University of Colorado at Boulder. "Your brain on imagination: It's a lot like reality, study shows." *ScienceDaily*, December 10, 2018. Accessed May 28, 2025. https://www.sciencedaily.com/releases/2018/12/181210144943.htm

unpaid bills, a leaky roof, the fight you had with your boss—or regretting that episode of infidelity, the job you didn't take, the awful thing you said to your mother five years earlier—that's where the pain lies and what brings us out of the present.

Rick's courageous response to his illness made me realize the time had come to write the book I had been thinking about for so long. Because he had invested the time and energy in developing a comprehensive Life Plan, he was able to fully embrace the present moment. He was at peace with a devastating diagnosis. The lessons I had learned from working with clients who previously had spent much of their time engaged in worry or regret could help others lead lives more centered on the joys of now—on planning for the future rather than worrying about it and forgiving themselves for the past, rather than beating themselves up for things they couldn't change. I hope that, by teaching **Lifeonomics**, I can help some people free themselves from the suffering of constantly living in the past and the future. If you are caught up in worry or obsessing over the past, this book can give you some Life Tools to pull yourself out of that and turn your attention to life as it is today.

Lifeonomics is built around the Ten Agreements of Breaking Free of Worry and Regret, which are the foundational concepts of this book. I recommend taking your time and reading each one carefully, and letting it sink in, because the Ten Agreements build on each other.

They are:

1. Obsessing over that which we can't control is futile.
2. Worry is uselessly obsessing over a future we cannot control.
3. Regret is uselessly obsessing about a past that we cannot change.
4. There are only three things we can control: Our own Thoughts, Words and Actions.

5. We only have that control in the Present Moment.

6. We take control of our Thoughts, Words and Actions first by controlling our attention, and later through the use of Systems, Strategies and Structures.

7. Assembling a Life Team of people we trust is essential.

8. Creating a Life Plan that we believe in will help us stay focused.

9. Accessing the right Life Tools will help us build the skills we need.

10. We learn from the past and plan for the future so we can live powerfully in the present, free of worry and regret.

Mike's Lesson

Mike was an executive in the accounting department of a large company in our area. He was tall, slim and completely sure about almost everything. He was his wife Nancy's one true love, and they had raised two wonderful children together. At 55, he attended a University of Arkansas continuing education course on retirement that I taught. He came in to see me at my office after that, completely sure that he had to work for another five years, until he was 60, before he could retire. However, through some advanced tax and retirement planning, we were able to help him retire within a few weeks. Mike lived what he called five of the best years of his life. Sadly, within a couple of months of his 60th birthday, he was diagnosed with a terminal illness and died a few months later. How valuable do you think those five years were to him and the people who loved him?

The lesson I took from Mike's story is that time is our most precious asset. It is more important than money because we can almost always find a way to get more money, but when we're out of time, we're out. If our sole focus is on the chores and to-dos on our list, and we are constantly distracted by worry and regret, we can become complacent about the preciousness of every moment. No one lies on their deathbed and says, "I wish I'd made more money." However, it is easy to forget that we are only here for a finite time, and each day is miraculous.

There are three ways that we define *life* in our coaching methodology. The simplest is the time between our birth and our death. All we really have when we enter this life is the time until we leave it. Being aware of this truth (but not fearing it) is one of the greatest gifts anyone can ever receive.

The second definition of life is the *quality* of what we do with our time on earth. Life is about the meaning and purpose of what we do with our time, and we don't have to cure malaria or build hospitals in Ghana to live a life built around both. Meaning and purpose don't need to have high-flown religious or philosophical aspects. Simply doing our work to the best of our ability, with a spirit of service, and treating our loved ones and neighbors as we wish we were treated, can put us on the path to meaning and purpose.

In **Lifeonomics**, quality of life means *the percentage of a person's time left on this earth spent doing only what is Truly Important to them with the people who are Truly Important to them. In today's modern world, almost everything else can be either automated, delegated, or eliminated.*

A key phrase here in our methodology is "Truly Important." Over the years of advising and coaching clients, my team and I have found that what is Truly Important to each person can be vastly different. It's not our job to judge what should or should not be, but rather to find out exactly what that is for each person and help them build a life doing exactly that. There is an element of conscious choice to this. In the 35+ years of my career interviewing people about their lives, I have met people with great financial wealth but a terrible quality of life. I have also met people with very little financial wealth whose lives were rich, joyful and meaningful. Those with the best quality of life shared a mindset that supported this and the Systems, Strategies and Structures to make it happen. **Lifeonomics** is designed to teach you a system you can use for living a fully engaged life, the way they did.

What Is *Lifeonomics?*

Lifeonomics can show you how to replace *economics*, where everything is about money, with a mindset that will help you create a life you love through conscious choices in every moment that will help you to shed your fear of the future. It's a holistic approach to wealth planning that takes the money out of it, especially at first. Strange as this sounds, I believe wealth planning is about 10% money and 90% human nature and living life. While most brokers will want to talk with you about money and the stock market, *Lifeonomics* is built around asking a very simple question:

> *What would you change in your life if you weren't worried that you might regret the decision?*

Many clients in my wealth management practice tell me stories of a once-upon-a-time passion for golf, art, jazz, or travel and how they did the "mature thing" and gave up on that passion for the career that would allow them to make the most money. Then, once they retire, what do they do? They dive headfirst into the original pursuit that they loved dearly. When I see this, I want to shout, "Why didn't you just make a career out of what you loved in the first place?" But I don't because we can't go back in time. Unfortunately, many of us have been taught that putting money before our happiness is the only responsible way to live. Fortunately, we don't have to keep doing that. Our goal is to help everyone we can to live with more meaning, purpose, love and joy. That means dumping worry and regret and choosing to do something we like to call **Living Life²**.

The Four Types of Wealth

When you think about it, a wealth advisor often knows more about what's important to people and what they fear than their doctor, lawyer, rabbi, priest or pastor. (Maybe even their therapist.) I believe we have a responsibility to inform them that their lives are about more than money.

In *Lifeonomics*, money is merely one of several types of wealth:

1. **Intrinsic Wealth**: Time, talent, wisdom, education, health, our potential as human beings. This also includes such things as our capacity for love, compassion, patience and understanding, as well as one of my favorites: a sense of humor. Intrinsic Wealth is the sum of all that makes you…uniquely you.

2. **Relationship Wealth**: The most powerful way to manifest and experience our intrinsic wealth is by sharing it with others. These relationships can be with a spouse or life partner, family members, friends, our Creator, or whomever we choose, but they must be central. Given that it is not just what we know but often whom we know, Relationship Wealth also includes our list of business associates, acquaintances and the networks we may belong to, including our friends and followers on social media. Sometimes, having the number of a great plumber you know and trust can be priceless.

3. **Financial Wealth**: The sole purpose of money is to support and enhance the other two types of wealth. It has no other meaning. It is simply life's fuel. The trouble is that in many people's minds, financial wealth is the only kind. That's because of worry and regret. We worry about paying the bills and not having enough to live on after we retire. We regret past financial decisions and determine that we're going to earn as much as we can while the opportunity is there. So, money comes to dominate our lives, yet there never seems to be enough of it. We still worry, fear and suffer because money doesn't address what we really need: *The knowledge that we're living a life we can look back on at the end with pride and joy.*

4. **True Wealth**: This is all that money can't buy, and death can't take away. It is the result that takes place when we manage the first three types of wealth powerfully. That means trading worry and regret for peace, prosperity, passion and purpose, and spending our lives doing only what is Truly Important to us with the people who truly matter to us.

So, where does money fit into this? Money can be the blood that carries oxygen through a healthy life. Money can be freedom. Money can be potential energy. It's there to use as we see fit. And when we find the way to let go of worry and regret, and to spend our time doing what matters to us with people we care about—and when we have the help of a professional team that understands this—we very often find that somehow the money part falls into place.

You're not going to find a lot of information on things like stocks and bonds in this book. What you will find is a wealth of information on breaking free from worry and regret, some of it in the form of exercise worksheets. When you're ready to tackle them, go ahead and write in the book. Really. That's what it's for. We hope your copy will be dog-eared and filled with Post-its and paperclips because you've found so much you can use. It can be a powerful way to transform your life, and it's actually fun.

Oh, and our third definition of life? It's a series of connected precious moments that we're present to savor. Completely present, fully engaged and unattached to the outcome. That's what you can experience when you fully understand **_Lifeonomics_**. We call that **Living Life^2** {exponentially more fulfilling}. Ready for a new way of being? Let's get started.

– Rob Holdford

PART I:

WHAT CONTROLS YOUR LIFE?

CHAPTER ONE:

Don't Worry, Take Action

Worry is like a rocking chair—it gives you something to do, but it doesn't get you anywhere.

—Author Unknown

There are two ways of looking ahead to the future. One is to plan for statistically probable events, the way I do as a wealth advisor. For example, we have about a 24% chance sometime in our working life of becoming disabled and unable to work for some length of time, so it is important to at least consider building up a cash reserve and/or possibly getting disability insurance.[3]

And we will all die someday, making it wise to consider life insurance if we have a family to protect. When something is probable, it makes sense to create a strategy for it and base our actions on that strategy.

When we are obsessing about events that aren't probable, we are worrying, one of the two mental habits that blight our lives. This is the ***Lifeonomics*** definition of worry:

---

[3] *Council for Disability Awareness. (n.d.).* Disability statistics. *Disability Can Happen. Retrieved May 28, 2025, from* <u>*https://disabilitycanhappen.org/disability-statistics/*</u>

Useless obsessing over a future we cannot control.

For us, worry is more about the obsessing part, far past any real benefit, than the issue itself. We do believe that there are legitimate concerns in life that need to be addressed; however, **obsessing is not addressing.** Something qualifies as a legitimate concern only if we have some actual control over it. Let's talk more about control.

We have very little control over what will happen to us in life. There are really only two aspects of life that we can control: how we *prepare* for what *might* happen and how we *respond* to what *does* happen. How we prepare and respond determines a great deal about how our lives progress. For example, if someone finds out they have dangerously high cholesterol and starts losing weight and changing their diet, they're responding in a healthy, positive way. The alternative is denial. They could choose to hope for the best and keep right on eating pizza and prime rib. Even very rational people often respond to bad news or the possibility of it with denial. It's our mind's way of protecting us from things we'd rather not know. My job as a wealth advisor and life coach is to help people overcome denial so they can take the steps to protect themselves in the future.

Exercise: Worry Inventory

What are you worried about? List your worries here, along with your take on whether they're something you can prepare for or control. Rank them from one to 10, with one being the most worried. You can also download this worksheet at www.Lifeonomics.com.

Worry Inventory				
Worry	Rank 1-10	Legitimate concern? Y/N	In my control? Y/N	Can I prepare? Y/N

Learned Helplessness

People who practice chronic, debilitating worry tend to feel helpless in their lives and powerless to change anything, including themselves. This mindset robs them of the mental strength to deal with the normal ups and downs of life.

> *Let us be of good cheer, remembering that the misfortunes*
> *hardest to bear are those which will never happen.*
>
> *—James Russell Lowell*

Helplessness is learned from people who have the best intentions for us: our parents and caregivers. As babies, we can't do much for ourselves. If we are fortunate enough to have loving parents who take care of us, suddenly every need is met with nothing more than a cry or a pointed finger; we are taught that we are entitled to all the love, attention, food, clothing, shelter and healthcare that we need. Later, many children have parents who, meaning well, do incredible harm by giving their children "everything they didn't have growing up," which is what we used to call "spoiling kids rotten." At the same time, schools keep us ignorant of how money works and "bolster our self-esteem" by moving us up a grade even when we fail a class.

Well, self-esteem doesn't come from having your ego stroked; it comes from overcoming obstacles to achieving a goal. So, is it any wonder that many of us feel helpless to navigate life's mazes? Any failures we experience reinforce our helplessness.

Psychologist Dr. Martin Seligman developed a brilliant theory behind the concept of "learned helplessness," which identifies the most common habitual attitudes that contribute to feeling helpless versus feeling empowered. In his research, Seligman identified three main attitudes that define learned helplessness and learned optimism when people confront failure:

LEARNED HELPLESSNESS

1. **Personal** — *"It's all my fault."* This is the attitude of someone who decides they are responsible for what happened, no matter what caused the failure.

2. **Pervasive** — *"This sort of thing always happens to me."* This person sees the same weakness or shortcoming that caused this failure throughout his or her life.

3. **Permanent** — *"I'm never going to be able to change."* Someone with this attitude is resigned to the idea that whatever shortcoming was responsible for the failure cannot be improved upon.

LEARNED OPTIMISM

1. **Impersonal** — *"You know, stuff happens."* This person sees the cause of the failure as something at least partially outside their control.

2. **Isolated** — *"Just because I fell short in that venture doesn't mean I can't succeed in others."* The person does not spread the poison to other areas of life.

3. **Impermanent** — The person sees his or her weaknesses as surmountable. *"I'll learn from my mistakes and do better next time."*

It doesn't take a Ph.D. to see that learned helplessness is a recipe for worry. If we don't believe we can achieve success or change the qualities that bring failure, all we're going to do is worry. On the hand, learned optimism, in which we take responsibility for our mistakes but don't make them into the entire story, empowers us to take control of the parts of our life that we can control: Our Own Thoughts, Words and Actions. We learn to trust ourselves and our decisions and to let go of the rest. The best thing about learned optimism is that it can be *learned.* We can train ourselves to adopt these positive habits. I think it's a must for anyone who wants to live free of worry.

Exercise: How Do You View Failure?

How you respond to life's failures and setbacks has a lot to do with your success in life. How do you think you view failure now? What will that knowledge compel you to change about your attitude toward failure? Check the boxes that apply to your attitude. If you like, download this exercise from www.Lifeonomics.com.

How Do You View Failure?					
I tend to see my failures as:	Personal	Impersonal	Pervasive	Isolated	Permanent	Impermanent

What does this say about me?

Cancer of Probability

As a wealth advisor, it's not only my job to help people prepare financially for the probable events in their future but to help them get some perspective on what is likely—and very unlikely—to happen in the coming years. To put it another way, I teach people the difference between planning for the future and projecting into it. When we plan for the future, we take concrete action based on statistical probabilities. When people project events into the future, they ask what can be the unhealthiest of all questions: "What if?" The unknown nature of the future, which some people find exciting, can become a source of fear that spirals into the vicious cycle of endless worry.

I call this diseased thinking "cancer of probability" because it turns into obsessive worry over things that, in all likelihood, will never happen. People caught in a death spiral of worry lose all perspective on the probabilities of life. The fact is, life is a game of probability. The odds at any one time are very much in our favor. But worry blurs the line between *possibility* and *probability*. Is it possible that your headache is caused by a malignant brain tumor? Yes. Is it probable? No, it's very improbable. Is it possible that the airline flight you're on will be brought down by terrorists? Yes, but it's extremely unlikely.

People often only see the possibility of something, not the probability. The fact is, when I'm working with a client, it's irresponsible and probably unethical for me to create a plan for them to deal with something extremely unlikely to occur. All I would be doing is feeding their worry. Instead, I explain that while life can throw some curves at us through the years, the best way to respond with confidence is to prepare and have a secure financial foundation beneath us. Long-term care insurance can give you the confidence that if you ever need to move to an assisted living facility, your family will not be bankrupted by the staggering costs. Life insurance can make it easier for your family to maintain their lifestyle once you pass. Having a diversified investment portfolio can help protect you if world markets suddenly come crashing down, as they did during the Great Recession, or the government shuts down commerce as we know it, as we experienced during COVID-19. An honest assessment of probability and an action plan to deal with it are the mature ways to approach the future.

Actively Doing Nothing

Unfortunately, in our society, we have been sold a bill of goods that says, "Responsible and caring people are supposed to worry." NOTHING could be more wrong. Worry is a self-delusion that makes us feel like we're actively addressing a possible future problem when, in fact, we're doing nothing at all. Actually, we're doing worse than nothing. We're stressing ourselves out, probably driving the people around us crazy and hampering our ability to enjoy life.

Here's another definition of worry for you to chew on: *Worry is a loss of faith.* When we dwell obsessively on the possible bad things that might happen in the future, we're declaring that we don't have faith. If the worry is that something will happen to you, you're saying that you lack faith in your ability to cope, to keep yourself healthy, to manage your money wisely and so on. If the worry is about someone else, you're telling that person you think they're weak, foolish, or incapable. If you're a person of faith, you're basically telling God, "I don't believe you'll give me what it takes to cope with what comes."

Of course, bad things happen sometimes, but so do good things. However, our culture has taught us that thinking positively is childish! We're told that if we focus on the worst things that can happen in a situation, we're wise and realistic. If you talk with anyone who has visited the Dalai Lama or other Eastern mystics, they all tell you that if you can stay in the moment instead of worrying, you will enjoy child-like joy and positive energy. A child lives in the moment. Worrying is something we teach our kids to do by example. It's a habit that pulls our attention to the tiny probability that something bad will happen instead of the overwhelming probability that it won't. There is nothing of value in worry. Not a single thing. Worrying is a useless activity.

"Worry is like paying debt that you don't owe."

—*Mark Twain*

Planning Is Everything

Responsible adults substitute planning for worry, separating legitimate concerns from unfounded fears. They learn from the past, plan for what might go wrong and put mechanisms in place to respond well to those concerns should they come to pass. Those mechanisms are often financial and legal: insurance, investments, wills and power of attorney documents. Maybe they plan to maintain their health with a program of diet and exercise. Then, with their plans in place and a professional team monitoring them to make sure they adjust as life changes, they go about living their lives, enjoying today without worrying about tomorrow.

That's what we hope this book will inspire you—and everyone to do. Control the things you can control (your Thoughts, Words and Actions), take steps to reduce the probability of misfortune as much as you can (by eating better and exercising if you have a family history of heart disease, for instance), and then get on with the business of living. Bad things may still happen, but if you have done everything you can to prepare for them and minimize their likelihood, why worry about them? We've controlled what we can, so let the rest go.

Raised by a worrier mother, I had to teach myself to overcome my habit of ruminating. My response was to confront my fears. This included doing things that took me out of my comfort zone. I skydived, bungee jumped and skied black diamond runs that gave me vertigo. To help overcome my shyness, I took up acting in high school and became a public speaker early in my financial career. I found that facing my fears with action is much more powerful than living with worry.

You might expect that, as a wealth advisor, I see planning as the key to living a truly fulfilled life. You would be right. Sure, it sounds romantic to throw all of your possessions in an RV and take off to see the country with no job, no insurance and no means of dealing with the uncertain future, but that romance quickly fades when someone gets sick, the RV breaks down, or you simply hit age 55 with no desire to live on the road anymore, no savings and no job skills. My duty as a financial professional is to enable people to live their lives more fully, and I do that by creating plans that allow my clients to be spontaneous and creative with their lives while knowing that beneath them, like a safety net below a trapeze act, is their investment/insurance/legal structure, ready to catch them if something goes wrong.

Exercise: How Will You Plan for Disaster?

Planning is your only defense against the unpleasant surprises of life. In this exercise, describe how you would plan for the major possible disasters of life. Download this worksheet at www.Lifeonomics.com.

How Will You Plan For Disaster?					
Type of disaster, i.e., Medical	Financial preparation	Legal preparation	Safety preparation	Physical (property) preparation	Mental preparation

Worriers will do anything to escape their fears, sometimes even avoiding the facts of their situation. They won't go to the doctor for fear of what they'll find out, even if it might prevent a serious health problem down the line. They don't want to know how much is in their retirement portfolio because they're afraid that no matter what they've done, it won't be enough. They harbor the delusion that any new information will always be negative, and once they face the facts, they will have something to worry about. So, instead, they deny that the facts are even important. If they don't have to deal with the facts, they can remain in blissful ignorance forever.

The trouble with denial and delusion as a strategy is that we can't prepare for or prevent something from happening if we're ignorant of it, and if it does happen, we have no safety net. It's like that precancerous polyp the doctor would have removed from your colon if you had gone in for a screening when you were 55, like you were supposed to. If avoiding worry is more important than facing facts, maybe that polyp becomes cancer by age 70. If your company gives you a choice between early retirement and being laid off, and you've ignored your retirement planning for 20 years because you were afraid of facing some hard choices, what do you do when you find out you can't afford to retire? How does job-hunting at age 65 sound to you?

Part of the process of living without worry and regret is ridding oneself of denial and delusion. This means coming to grips with the following:

- The facts are very rarely as bad as our fears make them seem.
- Knowledge, even when it's scary, is always better than ignorance because knowledge empowers us to plan.
- Planning and knowledge eradicate a great deal of worry because when we "know the worst" and can create a strategy to deal with it, suddenly it's not so bad.

Stop Worrying, Start Planning

Before we can do all of this, we've got to let go of the habit of worry. Worry is an addiction, like alcoholism, and it has triggers. For example, market volatility triggers worry for many people. People react with worry when they don't have a strategy and a trusted team to help them stay on track. It's crucial to see worry as what it is: self-indulgence that makes us feel as though we're addressing the potential troubles of life head-on when what we're doing is robbing ourselves of the power to deal with what comes. Ironically, what we've found is that most of the time, the things that knock us down aren't the things we worry about, but the stuff that comes out of nowhere, like Rick's brain tumor.

One of the best ways to begin breaking a worry addiction is to get the help of someone who can see your distorted thinking for what it is. I had a client named Gloria who was under tremendous pressure when she showed up at my office. Her mother was in a nursing home. As her mother's sole caregiver, she was struggling to keep up with her job as a technical writer involved with scientific research. I was worried about the stress she was under. She was running on empty. She was single, so she didn't have a spouse to help lighten her load. She was literally selling art off the walls of her house to pay for her mother's care, and she told me she was borderline suicidal. She had what is known as "caregiver's stress syndrome."

Well, it turned out that her mom had a bunch of telecom stock that she had won 20 years earlier in a bingo game and was now worth about $350,000. I asked the daughter about it, and she told me that her mom didn't want to pay the capital gains on the stock sale. The daughter was a scientist, but even highly educated people may have a blind spot about money. In the end, I brought in some tax attorneys, who showed her how she could sell the stock without paying a lot of taxes on it, and she was able to use the proceeds to pay for her mother's care. A few months later, I got a two-page letter from her saying that we may have saved her life.

Once her mom passed, she was worn out. We sat down and reviewed her financial plan. My team and I were able to show her that, thanks to all the saving and investing she had done, she had the means to retire. She decided to do that. She initially turned her attention to doing volunteer grant writing in the field of nursing home rights, which she learned about when her mom was sick. Then, she turned her attention to helping the State of Arkansas, where she lives, and began writing grants for programs to fight opioid addiction. Gloria learned from having her mother in a nursing home how important it was to advocate for the elderly and less fortunate. As a retired person, she helped the state win more than $100 million in grants for no charge and helped to save an untold number of lives. Now in her eighties, she is still a client and "extended family".

Another client and his wife had an $800,000 investment portfolio at another wealth management firm. He retired before 9/11. After that disaster, the market plummeted, and the couple's portfolio lost approximately $300,000 in value. The man became obsessed with this and developed an addiction to checking his portfolio daily. If it was up, he felt good; if it was down, he was depressed and miserable. Well, the market is up on a day-by-day basis only about 50% of the time, so half the time, he felt bad. Professionals know that we get most of our real returns in the market on only a few trading days a year; the rest of the time, we gain some and lose some. Basing your emotional equilibrium on your portfolio's performance is like basing your self-image as a sailor on the direction of the wind. When this couple became our clients, we looked at their entire range of financial needs and created a plan that helped ensure that no matter what happened, they would get by. They wouldn't be staying at the Ritz, but they would survive. The husband was finally able to put the worry burden down.

Are you a planner or a worrier? Here's a quick test to help you find out:

Planner	Worrier
You'd rather get all the facts so you can deal with whatever needs to be dealt with.	You'd rather not know the facts because you fear the unknown.
When you receive an unexpected communication, you don't think twice about it.	When you receive an unexpected communication, you assume it's bad news.
Problems motivate you to plan for a solution.	Problems confirm that there's something to worry about.
You're able to step back and keep life's challenges in perspective.	You're easily overwhelmed by what life's challenges *mean* (that you're unlucky, doomed, etc.)
You trust the professionals who are part of your team.	You don't trust anyone who tells you what you don't want to hear.
You're willing to change your plans to create a better outcome.	You cling to your worry-empowering habits like a drowning swimmer clings to a flotation device.
You have confidence.	You have little confidence.

Lifeonomics can be your key to living free from the worry that debilitates so many people. When set the habit of worry aside by shifting to planning, we'll find new worlds opening. In our practice, one of my great pleasures is helping people retire early. Often, they worry that retirement may never be possible, but with proper retirement planning, we can often show them that they can retire sooner than they think. Well, what do you get when you take someone in their fifties who's coming from a high-stress job and turn them loose at the peak of their experience, wisdom and knowledge? I've seen clients write novels, become lobbyists, go on missions around the world and more. Letting go of worry allows most people to realign themselves with who they really are. When we do this, life becomes a series of joyful moments. We no longer feel we have to sacrifice to survive. How might you realign your life?

Summary

- Worry is useless obsessing over a future we cannot control.
- We can learn to feel either helpless or empowered.
- It's important to know the difference between what's possible and what's probable.
- Worrying creates the illusion of doing something and being responsible.
- Worrying is a useless activity.
- Emotionally mature people plan instead of worrying.

To-Do List

- Ask yourself how often you worry about unlikely events.
- Look back to see how your pattern of worrying developed.
- Review any life planning you have done so far.
- Keep a journal and record your successful shifts from worry to planning.

CHAPTER TWO:

Forget Regret

We must all suffer from one of two pains: the pain of discipline or the pain of regret. The difference is discipline weighs ounces while regret weighs tons.

—*Jim Rohn*

My friend and client, Jeanie, was not close to her dad when she was growing up. He was something of a workaholic and was away from home a lot. As an adult, she realized there was a lot she didn't know about her father. As she reached her early fifties, she wanted to get to know him. They spent a lot of time together, and she asked him to share all of his stories. She found out about things he had done in his life that she had never known about. Their relationship became closer than ever.

Shortly after they reconnected, her father died. The funeral was on a Monday, and by Wednesday, Jeanne was getting worried. She called a friend and said, "I should be more upset. Why am I not grieving more?" The friend said, "You spent time with him, and you don't have any regrets about it." Some people might say, "How tragic, she had just gotten close to her dad." But she had no sadness about unfinished business because she had caught up. She was complete with her father.

Living In Reverse

Just as worry is obsessive attention paid to what could happen in the future, regret is obsessive dwelling on a past that we cannot alter. By definition, the past is beyond changing. What is done is done. Yet, I see many people sitting in my office punishing themselves over the mistakes of the past: the relationships they didn't pursue, the financial decisions they wish they could undo and so on.

Regret is a time machine that propels us backward and forces us to relive our errors of commission or omission again and again. Why spend time wallowing in what's done and gone while denying the lives we're leading now? Regret is just as unhealthy as worry.

"When one door closes, another opens; but we often look so long and so regretfully upon the closed door that we do not see the one which has opened for us."

—Alexander Graham Bell

Imagine that you work in an office. You've made a mistake that caused a problem for a client. You decide that to solve it, you need to go back into the file storage room and pull an old file. (I know most people don't have paper files in rooms anymore, but it still makes a good story.) The file storage room has no air conditioning, and it's August in Arkansas (an ugly, humid month). Imagine going into the horrible heat, pulling the file out, and getting the information you need to solve the problem. However, the file contains the blow-by-blow details of what led to the situation. You become so obsessed with the rest of the information in the file that you never come back out of the file storage room. You stay there in the heat, obsess and suffer, and never emerge to solve the problem that brought you there in the first place. That is how regret robs us of our lives. We develop a terrible, almost masochistic fascination with the sad facts in the file of our lives, beating ourselves with them endlessly.

But why do we continue to punish ourselves like this? In our justice system, a criminal cannot be tried and punished for the same crime more than once. The Constitution forbids what's called "double jeopardy." But we do this to ourselves all the time.

Now, it's understandable to feel bad about something we've done in the past, especially when it has hurt someone we care about. But it's clear to me that the kind of corrosive regret that lasts for years, or even decades, is something else: *punishment by guilt*. When I was wallowing in a deep pool of guilt and regret over a painful divorce, a mentor said to me, "Guilt is just an excuse to do nothing and feel self-righteous about it." In other words, I believed that to be a "good" person, I had to feel guilty. It was as if rolling around in a pool of self-imposed guilt made me righteous. At that moment, my perspective shifted. I realized that I was swimming in a pool of guilt as a means of punishing myself for my sins, real or otherwise. I have spent a great deal of my life feeling guilty as a way to make myself do better, but I realized in that moment that you can drown in guilt.

Regret and guilt are only valuable in two ways:

1. We learn from them. The only good reason to look back into the past is to Learn From It! What else can we do? We cannot change what we've done. All we can do is try to see the patterns and decision points that led to it and make better choices in the future.
2. We use them as a rumble strip. At **Lifeonomics**, we believe guilt is supposed to be the rumble strip on life's highway, not a lane. When we get off course, the rumble strip makes a big noise. We quickly self-correct and get back on course.

Regret leads to guilt for many of us, as certainly as spring leads to summer. But there's no payoff, no redemption, because there's no way to alter what's in the past. Guilt does not make you a better person! Christ taught that we should turn away from guilt, just set it down and walk away. He knew it was a trap for the spirit. This is an idea that transcends any faith. Nonetheless, we hold onto it and its twin, regret, as a way of paying for bad calls and foolish actions. What we need to learn is self-forgiveness, but that's not the territory of this book. That's more suited to a therapist or a pastor.

Exercise: Regret Inventory

What do you regret today? Use this exercise to clarify your regrets from relationships, lost opportunities, or other life events and assess the importance of each, with one being the most important. (If you'd rather not write in the book, download the worksheet from www.Lifeonomics.com.) The point of this exercise is not to wallow in regret, by the way. Human beings have a tremendous capacity for change, and taking stock of your regrets can help you make decisions that will help you create a different future. (Later in the book, we'll help you with a regret-burning exercise.)

Regret Inventory				
Regret	Rank 1-10	My responsibility? Y/N	What can I learn from it?	Can I let it go? Y/N

Deciding is Suffering

My goal is to help people live without worry and regret, planning for and enjoying their futures to the fullest. For clients who get caught up in regret and indecision, I offer an option: not to decide. I give them the pertinent information, keep them informed about their choices and then tell them that we are going to decide not to decide for a while. In my practice, my team and I use the ***Lifeonomics*** Wealth Management System, which we have developed over the past 30+ years. It's based on the time-honored financial planning process of:

- Discovery
- Analysis and plan development
- Implementation
- Review.

Because of this system, clients don't need to make decisions until we have complete information about their financial situation, their goals, what they care about, the markets and so on. What we can do is make it okay not to decide until it's time. Clients can defer decisions on when to retire or how to allocate their assets until they're more comfortable. They can avoid the pain or at least stop associating the act of choosing with pressure. However, eventually, we often reach a point where a decision is unavoidable because of life events such as marriage, divorce, a layoff, or a death in the family.

Fortunately, by that time, we know them well enough to guide them as they commit to a course of action.

Exercise: What Is Truly Important To Me?

This is one of the two most important questions you can ask, and if you don't know what is important to you, now is the time to figure it out. One way to determine what is important to you is to track your activity for every hour in a given week and see how you are spending your time. If you say spending time with family is Truly Important to you, but you work 80 hours a week and travel three weeks out of the month, you are living out of sync with what matters to you and will need to make changes to avoid painful regrets down the road. As you reexamine what is Truly Important to you, be sure to choose current priorities, not just hand-me-downs. Ask yourself if this is still Truly Important.

Download this exercise from www.Lifeonomics.com.

What Is Truly Important To Me?
What's Truly Important to me?
Why is it important?

Note: You may need to ask and answer these questions several times to arrive at accurate answers. When you feel complete in your work, place your answers in priority order from most important to least important.

Do Your Best and Let It Go

Complete self-awareness of what we want and what matters to us is the key to living more fully. Our measure for a quality life bears repeating: *spending as much time as you can doing what is Truly Important to you with people who are Truly Important to you.* That's it. There's nothing magical about that statement. It simply depends on what speaks to your passion. Money is simply the energy source for that life.

If you are fully aware of what fires your passion for living and you live fully engaged with it, then you will always make decisions that serve you. If your passion is your family, and you turn down a job that would have paid more money but taken you away from your kids, you will never regret saying no to the position. If you have a passion for archaeology and decide to participate in a dig in Egypt but will be spending that time away from your spouse, you won't regret it because you'll come back so engaged and joyful and full of life that your relationship will be better than ever. Passion drives out regret.

However, to live this way, you must be aware of what and who matter to you most. We're not used to thinking in this way. Because we focus so much on money as an end, not the means to an end, we forget that we're supposed to be living, not just earning. Once again, let me remind you that the most important questions you can ask are: "What is Truly Important to me?" and "Who is Truly Important to me?" Once you know those answers, you will always strive to make your life what you want it to be.

When I was a child, my mother made sure we never missed Sunday school. But on one particular Sunday, Dad had gotten in late from his job as a locomotive engineer, so she decided to let us sleep in.

I was almost three years old at the time. My older brother Nate was eight. From what I've been told, he worshipped the ground I walked on. I learned to walk very late because he carried me so much. He was the closest person in the world to me.

Nate got up before the rest of us and asked if he could go next door to play with his best friend, Randy, as he had done a hundred times before. Randy was 12 years old. My parents said yes. What they didn't know was that Randy's parents weren't there. They had gone off to run an errand. This wasn't unusual back in the Seventies.

What also wasn't unusual in the South, to this day, was for Randy to get his first gun for his 12th birthday. We're hunters here. Randy's first gun was a shotgun, and he wanted to show it off. When he got it out to show it to Nate, it accidentally went off and killed him.

Randy came running over to our house beside himself, and my dad got up and ran over to the house. My father's eight-year-old was lying there with a slug through his head, gone. I'm imagining this based on what I heard second-hand. Dad wouldn't talk about it. I imagine him falling to the ground, holding his son and crying.

Mom, who was always very intuitive, sensed something was wrong. She grabbed me and started to cross the front yard. "Joe, what's wrong?!" she called to my father.

My dad heard her and did something I don't know if I could do. He got back up and met us halfway across the yard. There was no way he was going to let us come in and see what he'd just seen. So, he told Mom what happened instead.

After that, the coroner came. My mom and dad, both passionate Christians, went next door that same day. Mom pulled Randy onto her lap and told him they knew it was an accident. It was an amazing act of love and compassion. From what I'm told, I walked the house for months after this, calling for my brother. When I'd ask where my brother was, they'd say, "He's with Jesus."

"Well, tell Jesus to send him back," I'd tell them with a pooched lip and a stomp.

Still, it took years for my mother to let go of the belief that if she had only taken us to church that morning, her eight-year-old son wouldn't have been taken from her. She was able to forgive God, but forgiving herself and letting go of the regret took longer. No doubt it was healing when she had my younger brother, Joel. I remember the day she brought him home from the hospital. I was four years old. I climbed up on the couch, eagerly standing on my tiptoes to see into the crib and meet my "new little brother." Dejected, I stomped and puckered my lip again, "But he's so little. How am I going to play with him?!" Fortunately, he did grow. And we did play. For that matter, I guess we still play together, over 50 years later, and I thank God for him every day.

Our mom worried about Joel and me pretty much every day until she passed away, but she lived remarkably free of regret. Her strength and faith were humbling to me.

Fast forward, and I'm eight years old, and my grandmother gives me a bicycle that's too big for me. It's purple, with a banana seat and butterfly handlebars. And it does not have training wheels.

My dad is home and decides to teach me to ride it. And we have a really long driveway that slopes down. So, I hop on the bike. There is one problem. I don't know how to work the foot brakes very well. The driveway has a pretty steep decline toward the house. I pick up speed but cannot stop. I hit a step in our carport, and I fall all the way into the open storage room. I am hurt, humiliated beyond belief and crying my eyes out.

My dad comes over, looks and makes sure I haven't broken any bones. "Son, you lay there and cry all you need to, but in our family, we don't give up," he says. "We get back up." Remember, this is coming from the man who "got back up" after holding his dead son in his arms a few years earlier. So I get back up. I learn to ride that bike. And today, cycling is one of my greatest passions.

In that moment, Dad taught me the secret to living without regret. We might make a mistake or have an accident and inadvertently hurt ourselves or someone else. But, in every moment, we would have a choice: We could decide we still had things to do and get back up. Or we could give up. It would be one or the other. We call it the "**G Cycle of Life:**"

Get knocked down. **G**et back up. **G**et stuff done.

Rinse and repeat.

There are two days in the week about which and upon which I never worry...yesterday and tomorrow.

—*Robert Jones Burdette*

Exercise: Who Is Truly Important To Me?

The second essential question you can ask is about who you want to spend your time with, doing those things that are so important to you. Now is the time to think about such things. Here again, taking inventory of whom you spend your time around for every hour in a week will give you an idea of the leading players in your life. You can't change your boss or colleagues unless you switch jobs or start a business, but you have a lot of decision-making power about whom to spend your time with outside of work. If you say your spouse or life partner is the most important person in your life but you seldom spend any one-on-one time together, this could be an opportunity to change things. Download this worksheet at www. Lifeonomics.com to take stock.

<table>
<tr><td align="center">Who Is Truly Important To Me?</td></tr>
<tr><td>Who is Truly Important to me (individual number one)?</td></tr>
<tr><td>Why is this person important?</td></tr>
<tr><td>Who is Truly Important to me (individual number two)?</td></tr>
<tr><td>Why is this person important?</td></tr>
</table>

Moving Ahead

Some people trust their past decisions for better or worse and see mistakes as a source of growth and wisdom. We try to help all of our clients join this group. Although they sometimes experience regret, it is temporary, much like the feeling of failure we discussed when we talked about learned helplessness. It's okay to have regrets about something that happened in the recent past, as long as you pass through regret, analyze why you did or said something and gain insight that helps you move forward and let it all go, content to know that, whatever happened before, you did your best in the situation.

It is possible to free yourself from regret and to take full control of those aspects of your life that you can change. We'll explore how in the next chapter.

Summary

- Regret is the obsession over a past you cannot change.
- The only value in guilt is learning or being awakened to the need to act.
- Deciding is suffering because we worry that our decisions will lead to regret.
- We regret what we have not done more than what we have done.
- A quality life is spending your time doing what is Truly Important to you with the people who are Truly Important to you.

To-Do List

- Pick one regret and forgive yourself for it.
- Pick something you feel guilty about and figure out what you can Learn From It.
- Take a looming decision that's causing you to worry and set it aside for a while.
- Do something in the next 30 days that you have been regretting not doing earlier.

CHAPTER THREE:

What We Can Control

"You cannot control what happens to you, but you can control your attitude toward what happens to you, and in that, you will be mastering change rather than allowing it to master you."

—*Brian Tracy, Motivational Speaker and Author*

In his book, *The Four Agreements*, Don Miguel Ruiz puts forth the insight that everything we do and are is determined by the "agreements" that we make inside of ourselves about the world and the people around us. Here are a few of the areas of our lives that are affected by the life decisions that Ruiz believes we all make:

1. Who we are.
2. What everyone else is.
3. How to act.
4. What is possible.
5. What is impossible.

That's real wisdom because it makes clear that virtually everything in our lives is a result of the choices we make. We reach a compact, a treaty, with the rest of humanity about what we will do and how we'll do it, and that agreement decides our identity. If you and the world agree that you're a weak person who can't stand up for yourself, then your behavior and everyone's response to your behavior will only confirm that. On the other hand, if the agreement is that you're strong and indomitable, guess what. That agreement becomes a self-fulfilling prophecy.

In this context, it's clear that the only way we can live the lives we deserve is to make choices that evoke our greatest strengths and define not only how the rest of the world perceives us but also how we perceive ourselves. The only possible decision is a simple one: *Control the things we can control and quit worrying about the things we cannot control.*

The Foundation of Life

We often think we have control over all aspects of our lives that are beyond our power. For instance, many people believe that by making sound investment decisions, they can control the rate of return on their investments. They forget that the performance of financial markets and the larger economy, which are completely out of our control, also have an influence. Loyal employees often believe that if they work hard and maximize their value to their employers, they won't have to worry about being downsized, when, in fact, the value employees produce often has little effect on whether they will be let go when the time comes to cut costs. What does matter is how big their salary is. If employers believe it is too costly to keep them on payroll, they will be out of a job. These are just a couple of the areas of life where we have zero control. Thinking about that lack of control is understandably terrifying, so we tend to deny it.

A lack of awareness of what we can and can't control creates a state of constant anxiety for some people. For example, many people are more terrified of flying than driving, even though there are over 40,000 deaths each year from auto accidents in the U.S. That compares to about 360 deaths from aviation-related accidents, even with thousands of civilian aircraft flights per day from U.S. airports.

This means we are far more likely to die in an automobile accident than in a plane crash. People often feel a greater sense of control when driving because they're at the wheel and can see what is going on around them and react accordingly. But when we look a little deeper, it's clear that even when we're behind the wheel, we can't prevent every hazard that other drivers who may be impaired or distracted might cause. In contrast, when we're in a plane, we're relying on rigorously trained aviators guided at every step by a ground system dedicated to safety. On a plane, we have no control.

If we turbulence, all we can do is hold on and watch the flight attendants to see if there is panic on their faces.

> *If you see ten troubles coming down the road, you can be sure that nine will run into the ditch before they reach you.*
>
> *—Calvin Coolidge, 30th president of the United States*

Attitude and Perspective

Let's focus on what we can control: Our own Thoughts, Words and Actions. They all occur in the moment and are part of a larger tapestry that becomes the pattern of our lives. Eventually, these become *habits*, and whether we want to admit it or not, our habits—our patterned, unconscious ways of thinking, speaking and acting—drive much of what our lives turn out to be. **Lifeonomics**, perhaps more than anything else, is about changing our habits, regaining control over those unconscious patterns, and consciously changing them for the better.

The habitual patterns of Thoughts, Words and Actions that form as we get older and more set in our ways lead to a *perspective*, the "frame" through which we see the world. Everyone has a perspective, a sort of big-picture idea of how reality works and affects them personally. Some people's perspective is that life is unfair, and nobody wins. Others may feel that money is the only thing that matters or that everything functions according to a divine plan. There are as many perspectives of the world as there are people. Perspective is notoriously difficult to change once we reach a certain age. It can harden like concrete over the years, and it often takes something dramatic—a near-death experience, a divorce, a mental break-down, to bring on the epiphany that makes us reexamine our perspective and ask, "Is this really how I want to live?" Millions of people who suffer from addictions around the world often have to hit "rock bottom" before a transformation can truly begin.

With the help of a friend and mentor, I had a major epiphany not long after my first marriage broke up. I discovered my life's purpose: To inspire and empower myself and others to overcome adversity, live powerfully and love unconditionally. Without that traumatic event in my life, this may never have happened. It changed my future. Shifts in perspective can be very powerful. I know they were for me.

Exercise: Controlling My Thoughts

Thoughts are one of the three aspects of life that we can control. What are your most common thoughts, the thoughts that crop up habitually? Do they produce positive results in your life or bring you harm? What can you do about it? If you want to write more, download this self-test from www. Lifeonomics.com.

Controlling My Thoughts			
My habitual thought	Positive or negative?	Can I change it? Y/N	How will I change it?

Exercise: Controlling My Words

Your words stem from your thoughts and go a long way toward programming your mind for better or worse. What are your habitual phrases or word choices, and how do they affect your life? If you're not sure what your catchphrases are, ask your family if you can record a dinner table conversation and listen to your speech. If you notice harmful verbal habits like giving unsolicited advice, holding people accountable without a prior agreement, or using the word "should" instead of "could," what can you do to change them? In case you're wondering why "should" can be such a harmful phrase, it is because it is an alert word that someone has likely coerced or manipulated you into what you are about to do. Turning a "should" to "could" changes the entire tone of the conversation.

Controlling My Words			
My habitual word or phrase	Positive or negative?	Can I change it? Y/N	How will I change it?

Everything Flows Downstream

While our Thoughts, Words and Actions drive our attitudes, the energy flows the other way as well. Our attitudes determine what we think, say and do. This is why it is so difficult to change without some kind of traumatic event. Everything we do reinforces the attitudes we've embraced. But if your mindset is built around worry and regret, does that mean you're stuck being that way unless you die on an emergency room table and are lucky enough to be brought back, or if you hit rock bottom because of an addiction? Of course not!

The way to shift our attitudes and escape worry and regret is to change our perspective, meaning our big-picture philosophy about life. A change in perspective, such as an atheist becoming a born-again Christian, is the most powerful thing that can happen to someone. If that sounds like a tall order, it is. You don't just say, "I'm going to start being positive about all people!" and do it. We're fighting an uphill battle against the weight of our habitual attitudes and patterns of thinking. They're programmed into our brains like computer code, so to change our perspective, we must *reprogram the computer*. We do that by—and here's where we come full circle—controlling our Thoughts, Words and Actions. Everything flows downstream from there.

However, to initiate the reprogramming process, we need to experience something known as *metacognition*, a term first introduced by psychologist J. H. Flavell in 1976. It means having the awareness to step back and watch yourself think, then see the patterns behind your behavior. In layperson's terms, it means three things:

1. Identifying what your perspective on life is.
2. Seeing the negative patterns in your Thoughts, Words and Actions (self-defeating, money-focused, envious, etc.).
3. Understanding how those patterns affect your perspective and your life in general.

Sure, that's a tall order. But you can do it. You're already doing it. Reading this book, especially this chapter, is the first step to unlocking and transforming your Thoughts, Words and Actions—to taking control of what you can control. So, let's dig more deeply into those three vital components of a life well-lived.

Attention!

Our thoughts seem hard to control because the stream of consciousness is going on inside our heads 24/7. But I'm not talking about controlling every stray thought that pops out of your subconscious mind like a soap bubble. I'm talking about controlling your *attention*.

So, what exactly is attention? It is the action of your thoughts being directed toward something or someone. I like the analogy of our attention being our mental flashlight. When someone or something captures our attention, that's like grabbing our flashlight. If you're not sure where your attention is directed, ask yourself, "Who's got my flashlight?" Controlling your thoughts is a matter of commanding your attention, making attention a conscious act, not something that's reflexive and reactive—essentially grabbing your own flashlight.

Understanding these three types of attention will help you achieve this and gain better control over your thoughts.

1. **Moving attention:** This is the hummingbird of mental activity, zipping from place to place, never slowing down or stopping for long. Our attention ricochets off things and people, bouncing around like a pinball, lighting on things without being captured by them. Moving attention is something that takes place when we are too busy to govern our thoughts, like when we're attempting to multitask while scrolling on a smartphone, or worrying about 100 things at once. It robs us of our ability to think proactively or assess our responses to things because there's no mental bandwidth left.

2. **Captured/emotional attention:** Captured attention allows people who are exerting no active control over their attention to sit for hours and focus. It's the kind of attention we pay as we watch a movie in a dark, air-conditioned room full of strangers. Emotion is the key to capturing attention because we all have triggers that capture our thoughts: guilt, lust, tragedy and so on. One of the most effective ways to capture attention is to tell stories, whether in a movie, a keynote speech, or at the dinner table. The emotional content of the story captures our attention and holds it. It is as if our attention is a flashlight

with a narrow beam. When our attention is drawn to something, we have a thought about it, and emotion is our body's reaction to the thought. That keeps us focused on whatever has grabbed our attention. Keep in mind that this is largely reflexive attention; we have little control over what triggers our emotions. So, if our emotions are mostly captured, then we have to ask, what or who is controlling our thoughts?

3. **Focused attention:** This is the ideal state to achieve. Here, we train ourselves to hold our attention on something that has not necessarily captured our emotions. For instance, if you've ever taken a yoga class, you probably focused your attention on a spot on the wall while doing the balancing postures.

So, now that you are aware of these three types of attention, ask yourself an important question: "Where is my attention right now?" Is it scattered among a dozen targets, engaged in a story you are reliving in your imagination, or focused on this book and how to put the ideas you are learning into action? The key to living free of worry and regret is to literally notice where your attention is and to understand that what you give your attention to becomes your truth. You buy it, you own it. This is the meaning of the term "to pay attention." Focused attention gives you the power to catch your attention wandering or being "hacked" and redirect it toward something productive and positive. One of Dr. Joe Dispenza's most famous quotes is, "Where you place your attention is where you place your energy."

This chapter is about what we can control, and nothing is more fundamental than controlling our attention. When we realize that our attention has been focused on something that isn't within our control, we can gently move ourselves back to the center of our power by refocusing on what is in our control. Can you find something to focus on when your attention wanders? Where can you bring your mind to recall what's important? My favorite place to focus my attention when this happens is to pull it back to what I am grateful for. This centers me and reminds me of where my attention belongs. The focus required to write this book showed me how much I have improved my ability to control my attention. If I can do it, anyone can do it!

This concept often comes into play in my practice as a wealth advisor. When I was working on the first edition of this book, the financial markets took a major hit in the Great Recession. As I update this version, millions of people are still recovering from a global pandemic and worried about their future. Time has marched on, but my advice has remained the same: to focus on the things they can control, namely, their decisions. In finance, rash decisions usually lead to disaster. So, when clients call me in a panic about headlines they've seen in the news, I remind them that we have already planned for this and have a strategy to deal with it, so there is no need to worry. With the world changing by the day because of technologies such as artificial intelligence, this mindset will be more important than ever in the future. Change can be distracting and anxiety-producing, but if you have a smart plan in place, it doesn't have to be—and you will be able to keep your attention focused on doing what truly matters to you with the people who truly matter.

When I really worry about something, I don't just fool around. I even have to go to the bathroom when I worry about something.
Only, I don't go. I'm too worried to go.
I don't want to interrupt my worrying to go.

—J.D. Salinger, *The Catcher in the Rye*

Affirmative, Sir

The words we speak have incredible power. They can be like fallout from the nuclear reactor of the mind. Even though our words are easier to control than our thoughts, some of us choose not to control what comes out of our mouths. Why? We usually believe that the words we say have no personal consequence for us. However, we hear our own words and can program ourselves to believe whatever we are saying. That is why it is important to "Be impeccable with your word," as we learned in *The Four Agreements*.

The fact is that what we say has the power to shape our thoughts. Thoughts become words, and words become action, but words also feed back into the mind to reinforce subconscious perceptions. If we continually tell ourselves how unattractive we are, we begin to believe it. Others hear it and do the same, and their response to us reinforces our own subconscious beliefs. The world is a great echo chamber for the words we say. Controlling our words can have a dramatic effect on the experiences we have in the world, so it is just as important as controlling our thoughts.

Fortunately, it can be easier because words come with the safety net of having to travel from our brain to our lips. How often have you thought something but not said it? That's an important habit to develop.

As you learn to control your words, certain types of speech have no positive value whatsoever. You may want to look out for:

- **Complaining** — In other words, whining. I'm not talking about voicing a legitimate concern about something. Rather, it is fruitless to be negative about things you can't control. Complaining serves no purpose other than to let other people know you're unhappy in the hope they will do something to fix the problem.

- **Doomsaying** — There's a certain type of person who, when presented with a scenario, will immediately tell you all the terrible things that can happen. The wife of a good friend, for example, decided to give birth to their second child at home with the help of midwives. Immediately, one of their friends launched into all the horror stories she had heard about home birthing. Perhaps she thought she was being helpful, but focusing on the potential harsh reality of someone else's choices seldom changes their mind and usually drives away the person whose plans they are judging.

- **Gossip** — One of the most destructive kinds of speech, gossip not only poisons the reputations of the subjects but also brands *you* as a gossip in the eyes of others. If you must talk about others, find something positive to say about them. If not, follow your mother's advice: if you can't say something nice, don't say anything.

- **Self-defeating talk** — When you talk about how bad things are or how hard a week you're having, you're persuading your subconscious that what you're saying is true. So, when people ask me how I'm doing, I like to repeat affirmations like, "I'm great and getting better." Every time those words come out of my mouth, no matter how often I say them, they influence me. For the same reason, when people ask me how work is going, I like to say, "Work is going great. Every day, I'm blessed with the chance to do what I do." This costs me nothing, and I don't care if the listener thinks I sound like a rah-rah cheerleader. It helps set me on a strong course and gives my mind an infinitesimal little nudge toward the positive. Remember, when you choose the words you use, you are programming yourself for good or bad, positive or negative.

As you look for more self-affirming phrases to use in your own life, remember that affirmations are rooted in positive thinking, not childish optimism. In my self-talk, I make it a habit of saying things like "I feel great" and "I am at peace." Being honest with yourself about the facts of your life doesn't mean you can't be as positive and life-affirming as possible! The words that come out of your mouth shape your thoughts and your progress through each day. They are the first step to manifesting results in your life. This sort of positive mental programming is often part of organized religion, as in Christianity's profession of faith, but it is helpful regardless of your belief system.

Be careful about repeating your affirmations at the top of your voice in a crowded elevator, but otherwise, go for it! Controlling your words not only makes it easier for your mind to believe what you're saying, but it reshapes your environment. If you show others that you're a positive person, their behavior will reflect that, and your subconscious will more readily believe what you're saying.

Exercise: Controlling My Actions

Thoughts and words lead to actions, and actions change our lives for better or worse. This exercise will help you identify actions that are constructive and destructive, allowing you to build on the positive ones that already exist in your life and eliminate the negative ones. Think about how productive you feel when you clean your entire home or bring in a cleaning crew, and it is sparkling and free of clutter. You want to feel that way about every aspect of your life, and controlling your actions is an important step toward that.

Use the chart below to list some of the habitual actions that shape your days. What habitual actions are controlling some aspects of your life? Working out every morning? Starting your day with prayer or meditation? Going to bed early enough to be well-rested every day? Eating or drinking too much?

Smoking? For each habitual action, ask yourself: Are your thoughts and actions constructive or destructive?

Very few people find that all of the actions they list on the exercise are constructive. Don't beat yourself up if you discover some of your habits are destructive. The point is to ask yourself, "What can I do about my destructive words and actions?" Look at each of them as an opportunity for improvement. Simply becoming conscious of a destructive habit, like devoting too much time to a toxic person who violates your boundaries, can be a first step toward making long-overdue changes.

You will probably find that as you fix on a bad habit, it becomes easier to change the others. For instance, quitting smoking can support you in your efforts to work out more regularly because it will be easier to breathe.

You don't have to do it alone. Finding outside support or an accountability partner can be essential to undoing hard-to-break habits, whether in your thoughts or actions. Ask yourself: Are there people who can help you prevent yourself from slipping into bad habits, whether that is finding a coach, exercise buddy, or support group? Are there structures you can put into place, like making a public commitment or cutting up your credit cards?

What if you mess up? Realize that the old you will resist change, and this may happen from time to time. Remind yourself that you have made a lifetime commitment to self-mastery. Then, pick up where you left off. This exercise is also available for download at www.Lifeonomics.com.

Controlling My Actions			
My habitual action	Constructive or destructive?	Can I change it? Y/N	How will I change it?

Create the Environment Needed to Succeed

Our environment can reinforce the thoughts and words we've been sending into the world. Ultimately, it will support us most if it reflects who we choose to become. If we want prosperity, we need to create an environment that fuels prosperity. Our office will ideally be a place where we can do our best work, and our home a sanctuary where we can refuel. Our physical world has the potential to take on the form of the ideal world we have inside our minds.

This also means choosing a lifestyle and surroundings that reflect our most cherished values. If health is our highest priority, then stocking our refrigerator with organic produce and taking a daily walk in nature may become a helpful part of our environment. If we wish we had the confidence that comes with not having debt, then we may want to pay off debts and stop running up new ones.

Beyond this, our environment also includes the people with whom we associate. The people around us reflect conscious choices. If we want to become more positive, filling our environment with positive people will support this. If we realize that too many of the people in our lives are negative, then it's important to remember we can change this, too. It's not difficult to do. We don't have to make the changes hurtful. Instead, we can gradually spend less and less time with those who bring negative energy into our lives.

Always keep in mind that our subconscious assumes that if a person is in our life, they must be reinforcing truths about us. Negative people reinforce the idea that our outcomes will be negative. People who are forever having problems and are asking us to bail them out reinforce the idea that we are somehow either everyone's white knight or just as messed up as they are. So, it's important to pay careful attention to our associations and be sure to control our thoughts and words. They will determine who comes into our lives—and who stays or leaves. If we're curious about who we are becoming, our associations might be the most revealing aspect.

Ultimately, everything begins with our thoughts. Exert control over them, and we will influence our words, which reach into the world and attract certain types of people to you. Those people will help us transform our environment, which, in turn, will guide our actions in a positive, confident, and prosperous direction. When our Thoughts, Words and Actions are working in concert to support us in living a life centered on the activities and people that truly matter to us, worry and regret will become obsolete. And we'll be ready to handle anything that happens that is beyond our control.

Summary

- All we can control are our own Thoughts, Words and Actions.
- Quit worrying about the things we cannot control.
- Planning and preparation—the things we can control—provide peace of mind.
- Attitudes influence Thoughts, Words and Actions.
- We can control our attention and what it falls on.
- Be careful of the words we speak, for they will shape our thoughts.
- Our thoughts will shape our habits and perspectives.
- Making sure our habits are constructive is essential to building a life we love.

To-Do List

- Make a list of the things we cannot control in our life.
- List the planning we have not yet taken to give ourselves peace of mind, break it down into steps and then begin implementing it to give ourselves peace of mind.

- Write some daily affirmations and start using them.
- Create a reminder system that helps focus our attention on what's important.

CHAPTER FOUR:

Break the Chains of Codependency

"We are finite creatures and must give as we decide in [our] heart to give (2 Cor. 9:7), being aware of when we are giving past the love point to the resentment point. Problems arise when we blame someone else for our own lack of limits."

– Dr. Henry Cloud and Dr. John Townsend, <u>Boundaries</u>

If you are over 40, you probably remember Blockbuster Video. If you are unfamiliar, the idea was that to watch a movie on demand, you had to go to the store and rent a video. If you were late in returning it, you had to pay an extra fee.

One night, a wealth advisor I know came home from work and decided he wanted to rent a movie. At the time, his practice was small. He was married with three teenagers at home, but was the only adult in the house who was working. The family had barely survived a series of tragedies over the previous couple of years, and his wife, who struggled with mental illness at the time, was self-medicating with alcohol. She would often call him in the office when he was with a client because she couldn't find the TV remote she had dropped under the bed or for other similar reasons. Although he was earning a solid income, they didn't yet have any savings, and he was worn out from the stress of supporting everyone. On this particular evening, he just wanted to rent a video and relax.

So, he headed to Blockbuster. When he went up to the window to check out his video, the clerk told him he had $180 worth of late charges. He hadn't rented a movie in months. These charges were his family's. The Blockbuster store was less than half a mile from where he lived, yet videos were piling up in the house.

He was seething. How could his family let the late charges build up like this when they knew he was working 60- to 70-hour weeks? He paid the late fees and then took everyone else's name off the account. In doing so, he took away the possibility of this ever happening again. He knew that certain family members might be upset, but he let it be what it was. He was done doing things he didn't want to do and paying for things he didn't want to pay for just to keep the peace. It was the only healthy way to respond. He was never again going to give someone else the power to spend his money without permission, even his family.

He didn't realize at the time that this seemingly minor decision to set financial and personal boundaries would contribute to the unraveling of his unhealthy marriage or that it would ultimately help him free himself of codependency. Codependency, in case you haven't heard that phrase, means making decisions solely to get others to like us or because we want to control them, even if it means hurting ourselves or disregarding our well-being. Sometimes, people become codependent because they're raised in dysfunctional homes, where they develop these behaviors as survival skills. Other times, codependency develops in adulthood. Anytime someone has been put in a position to be responsible for a grown adult who can't cope with the normal responsibilities of adult life for any length of time, it is incredibly common for the disorder of codependency to develop.

Oftentimes, this is because of mental illness or addiction. And almost any time there's an addiction, there are an addict and a codependent.

Both of them are equally sick. In some cases, the enabler is sicker, with an equally powerful addiction to the addict. Both people will need to work on themselves to return the relationship to health if it can be saved. In the wealth advisor's case, after extensive family and personal counseling, he determined that it couldn't be, and he and his ex-wife parted ways, though they did eventually heal their relationship and became close friends. They remained so until she died suddenly from a heart attack several years later at the age of 46.

In case you haven't guessed, the wealth advisor in this story was me. Anyone, including wealth advisors, can "fall asleep" and wake up one day to discover they are living a nightmare where it seems someone else is controlling their financial decisions and, consequently, how they spend their time. But who has control over any of us? No one but ourselves, as I came to learn. Blaming our lives on other people doesn't work well and is mostly not accurate. Even if a situation is someone else's fault, it's important to ask ourselves what we can control about it. There must be something. No matter how bad it is, we can still learn from it and get back to living in the now by learning to set appropriate boundaries, financial and otherwise.

The Path to Recovery

"I will live a lie without even knowing it, And I'll wonder why I'm not happy And why no one has ever thanked me."

— Stephanie Darnell, poet

When I work with clients who can't meet their financial goals despite all of the work we do together, they are often struggling with codependency issues. Sometimes, they have a hard time saying no to their spouse or children because they've been raised to believe that being a good provider is their highest purpose in life. Other times, they're in more complex situations where someone else is manipulating or coercing them to the point that they may fear that they'll be harmed by their abuser if they say no. These clients need professional help to turn things around.

All of these situations have one thing in common: They don't happen overnight. You've heard the story of the frog in boiling water. Most people who land in that pot don't just jump in. They haven't realized that the small decisions they made every day for months or years gradually brought the water to the boiling point. They only started paying attention when the water began scalding them.

But simply jumping out of the pot—obvious as that may look—isn't as easy as it seems if someone is codependent. Many of us need outside help to heal and develop healthier relationships with both the other people in our lives and our money. No amount of planning, saving and investing can help us if we don't have the tools in our toolkits to set healthy boundaries in our financial decision-making. For codependents, recovery means learning that we count, too, and that we must opt to live in a way in which we feel safe. It's about treating ourselves the way we treat other people.

Of course, that is easier said than done. Many middle-class people don't learn how to set financial boundaries because the world sets boundaries for them in the form of a weekly paycheck. Many live paycheck to paycheck, without cash reserves, especially in times of high inflation. The only boundary they know is not being able to afford something. That was the case when I was growing up. I remember my mom at the grocery store, who sometimes had to put things back because Dad's paycheck only went so far. Unfortunately, in today's world, many people have easy access to accounts like the one I had at Blockbuster and credit cards that they misuse at their own peril. Once armed with these potentially lethal weapons, they discover that they have weak muscles when it comes to setting financial boundaries—and find themselves struggling with debt and unhealthy relationships, which tend to go hand in hand.

The best way to get stronger is to find a group of people who have recovered, such as those in a 12-step program. This is known as peer coaching. If you're being abused, for instance, seek out a group of people who have been victims of the same type of abuse. It's very powerful to be guided and coached by someone who has gone through exactly what we are going through.

Groups like this can help us see our lives through a new lens. If we've been enabling an addict, for instance, we may be surprised to learn that our seemingly helpful behavior, whether it's paying our loved one's bills or making excuses for their absences from work, is making the addict worse. As I learned from Al-Anon, we must think carefully before intervening in the normal path people are on. When we go in and take someone's challenges away from them, it may look like we're helping them, but we may just be pushing out their rock bottom. Giving money to someone who's still drinking or using drugs, no matter what the situation, may lead to more drinking or drug abuse. It tremendous wisdom and knowledge to make healthy decisions in a situation like this. That's where groups like Al-Anon can help.

What if you are the one who is addicted? 12-step programs can be equally valuable. Addiction is not a problem that just goes away on its own. Drug and alcohol addiction will destroy everything they touch if we give them time. In the meantime, we will not be able to manage our finances in a healthy way if any untreated addiction—whether it's to alcohol, prescription drugs, shopping, gambling, pornography, food, or something else—is driving our daily decisions.

For some people, peer groups aren't the best fit, and private, professional help is better. Recovery can take time, and it's worth experimenting until we find the right help for our situations. One of the best investments we can make in our financial futures is getting help for any addictions and mental health problems that exacerbate it, such as anxiety or depression.

Making More Conscious Financial Decisions

One way to determine if we're in a codependent relationship that affects our finances is by understanding why we make the financial decisions we do. This is particularly true when it comes to decisions that involve other people.

There are three ways that someone else can influence us: persuasion, manipulation, and coercion.

- *Persuasion* involves making a case for our point of view with the goal of coming to agreement. *Agreement* involves having a discussion in which both parties come to alignment based on mutual respect for each other's point of view, and no one feels undue pressure to do something they don't want to do. As odd as this may sound, an agreement to disagree is still an agreement. At least we know where each other stands.
- *Manipulation* is using guilt or misinformation to get someone to do something.
- *Coercion* is forcing someone to do something. Identity theft is a good example of coercion. If someone, including a family member, opens up a credit card in our name that we end up having to pay off, that's stealing. Stealing, by its nature, is coercive. Threatening someone with violence or behaving in an aggressive way that makes someone fear that they'll be hurt is another form of coercion.

The only healthy way to come to an agreement about finances is through persuasion. That's especially true if we live in a community property state, where we could be held liable for a spouse's debts. If we're agreeing to pay for things we don't want to buy or spend money on because of manipulation or coercion, we need to put an end to it, or it will ruin our finances.

Breaking the Cycle of Codependency

When I was growing up, my mom had a thick paperback book on her nightstand called *When I Say No, I Feel Guilty*. It was an assertiveness training book. Unfortunately, I'm pretty sure she never read it and often got manipulated by people who took advantage of her good nature.

Like my mother, many of us never learn to say no as often as we should. We say yes to overly philanthropic ideas or helping one of our children get out of debt when we really can't afford it. Having a Life Team—a group of advocates who are invested in us and our well-being—can help us prevent this or nip it in the bud when we're tempted to make a decision that may hurt us.

A wealth advisor can be a key player on this team, helping us to bring clarity and accountability to our decisions so we don't make them in a state of denial and delusion. As wealth advisors, we can utilize advanced financial planning software to help us understand precisely how an individual's choices will impact their finances. At the time I was writing this book, a couple we work with wanted to withdraw 25% of their entire retirement savings to help a daughter with legal problems. We determined that the real cost of this was a 25% lower income for the rest of their life in retirement. That meant if they planned to get $4,000 a month, they would now receive $3,000. Armed with that information, they decided to go ahead with helping her out, even if it meant making personal sacrifices. Unfortunately, their sacrifice did not help. The daughter lost her case and went to prison anyway. Disappointing as that was, they did make their decision unprepared.

A wealth advisor can also help us say no to ourselves if we're easily tempted to spend any windfalls that come our way. When people who have not had money their whole lives receive a windfall, they often feel like they have a big pile of cash to spend. They don't realize that it should be viewed as an income-producing machine. If our machine is big enough, it can produce the income we need in retirement—but only if we keep the cash in our investment account. The right wealth advisor can help us avoid temptation and develop the skills we need to stay focused on our life's biggest goals, so we don't blow the money and then regret it.

People are often surprised when I say this, but our wealth advisor can also help us build a stronger marriage. Most of us are far too close to our own lives to see them objectively. That's particularly true with marriages. If a couple has been married for any length of time, there is a shift in the way they see each other. Sometimes, they stop listening to the other person. Familiarity often really does breed contempt. If one person is not working, they may be financially dependent on the other. Dependency often breeds resentment as well. A wealth planning team can help us put a plan together so we can break out of those patterns.

The main thing as a couple is to have an agreement about how finances will be handled in the marriage. What is the agreement? What are the values of the family? Who are the people who are Truly Important to us from a values point of view? What are we trying to accomplish in our marriage? What does it serve? The answers should be woven into our financial plans. People often get into marriages without any agreement about how they will live their lives, but that doesn't mean they can't find common ground.

Sometimes, the solution to problems like one spouse running up credit card debt is as simple as what behavioral finance experts would call peeling away the layers. When we pay for things on a credit card, it insulates us from the pain of making irresponsible purchases by delaying the impact. Shifting to paying for all purchases with cash, where we have to hand over the money, can make spending more real and can be done without a lot of extra work. In other cases, someone with compulsive behavior may need help from a 12-step support group. If you are looking for the right group for you or a loved one, check out the list in the Appendix.

"This isn't a death. It's a rebirth, an awakening as profound as the moment when sobriety first takes hold of the lifelong drunk… Are you willing to risk it? Have you reached the point where enough is enough?"

— *Melodie Beattie*

Knowing When It's Time for a Fresh Start

I'm a big advocate of counseling and coaching for people with codependent tendencies, but these services can only help us so much. No human being should stay in a situation where they are being abused emotionally, financially, or physically. If someone is doing this to us, it's not good for either person on a spiritual level. Sometimes, our decision to leave someone who is engaged in a cycle of destructive behavior is the only thing that will compel them to get the help they need. (If you are in a situation of coercive control or physical abuse, make sure you get help from professionals as you plan your exit. These situations can be dangerous.)

Learning how to set boundaries and break free from codependency can be challenging, but it's also a worthwhile effort that can clear space in our lives for better things. Although my first marriage came to an end, I now have a great marriage with my wife, Joy. We've put many "systems" in place to make sure we have a healthy relationship with money, including having regular discussions about the agreements that underlie our marriage. That never would have happened had I not let go of trying to control my ex-wife. When we're trying to control things that are out of our control, the situation—whatever it is—becomes dysfunctional. When I finally "Let Go and Let God," as Al-Anon advised, everything in my life changed for the better. That can be true for you, too.

Summary

- If you can't meet your financial goals despite the work you are doing with a wealth advisor, you may be experiencing codependency issues in one of the important relationships of your life.
- Codependency means making decisions solely to get others to like us or because we want to control them, even if it means hurting ourselves or disregarding our well-being.
- If you are codependent, it is important to work on changing your Thoughts, Words and Actions. We simply don't have the power to change another person.
- 12-step programs that offer peer support, such as Al-Anon, are a powerful tool for healing ourselves from codependency
- Never stay in a situation where you are being abused physically, emotionally, or financially. It is not good for either individual on a spiritual level. Seek the help you need to leave these relationships.

To-Do List

- Ask yourself if any of your financial problems stem from not setting appropriate boundaries in your financial lives in a codependent relationship.
- If you need help making changes to a codependent relationship, consider attending one of the 12-step peer-support groups listed in this chapter.
- If you feel you are in an abusive relationship, seek professional help to extricate yourself.

PART TWO:

THE "L STEPS"

CHAPTER FIVE:

Let It Be

"When I find myself in times of trouble, Mother Mary comes to me, whispering words of wisdom, let it be."

—John Lennon & Paul McCartney, "Let It Be"

Many years ago, I was vacationing with my family at a lodge on top of a mountain. My then-10-year-old stepson, Kevin, jumped onto a ledge well off the beaten track while he was playing without looking where he was jumping. He landed right on a poisonous snake sunning itself on a rock. Kevin screamed. The snake screamed. Okay, snakes don't scream, but it was obviously startled, and it instinctively bit Kevin several times in self-defense. This resulted in an emergency helicopter airlift and a stressful week-long stay at our local children's hospital.

Fortunately, Kevin recovered completely. After it was all over, it would have been easy to ask the Universe WHY this innocent child had to suffer or go on the warpath against snakes. I chose to Let It Be instead. The snake was just doing what snakes do. Kevin was just doing what 10-year-old boys do. He did learn a valuable lesson about hiking in the forest, but that was the end of it.

Let It Be, Learn From It, Let It Go

Let It Be is an incredibly powerful life tool that can change the quality of our lives almost immediately. It is part of a process we call the "L Steps" that can powerfully break old habits that rob us of so much of our time, attention, energy, and enjoyment. To quickly summarize, when you Let It Be, you accept the facts without judgment. Learning From It means making changes in response to what you observed. And Letting It Go is when we realize we've taken all that we can from an experience and stop dwelling on it. Once we Let It Be (Step One), we'll have the option to Learn From It (Step Two) and Let It Go (Step Three). Then we'll be able to Live Now.

When we know how to Let It Be, it gives us room to breathe before we progress to the next L Step. We then look to see if there is information from this experience or this encounter that will allow us to Learn From It. To Learn From It, we need to become conscious of the tremendous amounts of information coming at us. If we are unaware, it's very difficult to process the information and use what we learn to make changes in our lives.

It may come as no surprise that Learning From It is the step most people skip as they move right to fixing or complaining. But if we do take the time, we'll be ready for integration. Essentially, this is where we answer the question, "What do I do with this?" When we become conscious of all of the information coming at us, including the emotional information, we have the opportunity to absorb it, organize it in a way that we can re-access it, and apply what we've learned. The answer is to change our Thoughts, Words and Actions to shift our perspectives and the way we see the world—so we can Let It Go and Live Now.

Fully understanding what it means to Let It Be will help us get the most out of the drill down. L Steps, so let's Let It Be means to accept that we can't change other people's behavior and to stop trying.

We're not responsible for the actions or thoughts of other people, nor are we under any obligation to set them straight or prevent them from doing something that is hurting them.

Let It Be often means forgiving someone, but forgiving doesn't mean we have to put up with something that is hurting us. It doesn't mean failing to act on things we can control. If someone steals from us, we're not going to leave our money lying around for them to steal from us again. Having Systems, Strategies and Structures in place means we will have metrics in place to keep track of the facts. That will allow us to see the Truth with a capital T. We will be able to accept the facts of the situation, protect ourselves, and refocus elsewhere.

Let It Be means embracing the idea of metanoia, or turning away. We don't have to make our old life "bad" to turn away. We are simply being led somewhere else. Moving in a new direction is the difference between power and force. It reflects the idea that we can't force others to do things they don't want to do, and that we have a responsibility to ourselves and the people who love us to choose a life-affirming path for ourselves. Although we may have made a commitment to someone, such as marriage, we will not be able to enforce that covenant if the other person lacks honor and may harm ourselves by staying in the relationship.

Being able to Let It Be can help us live according to our purpose. If we have a North Star, outside stimuli or reinforcement won't affect us as much as the messages we are sending to ourselves. meantime, putting Systems, Strategies and Structures in place to help us master the things we actually can control can bring about dramatic improvements in our lives.

Sometimes, of course, it's hard to detach completely. If a loved one is hurting themselves, we may not be able to turn off all of our emotions about it. In those cases, I find it's helpful to accept the fact that I cannot detach completely and opt for "compassionate detachment," where I am invested in the outcome but still observing the situation at arm's length. Detachment is stepping over an alcoholic who has gotten drunk and fallen asleep on the floor, while compassionate detachment is taking time to put a blanket over them so they don't get cold as we head out to dinner with friends.

Let It Be can also be an incredibly powerful tool when we're dealing with behavior that irritates or infuriates us. While we can't control what someone else does, we can change our response to their behavior. In situations where I'm getting frustrated by someone else's behavior, I often ask, "What am I doing that is giving this other person power over me?" Then I stop doing it. People are going to continue on their natural path regardless of what we do. That frees us to take their actions at face value and respond accordingly—and to ask, "What can I learn from this?" Doing that makes us far less judgmental and patient about waiting for them to come to their own conclusions, if that is meant to happen.

This is often not easy. We're emotional beings, and it's difficult for us to divorce our feelings from the events of our lives. But when we can Let It Be, we are free to deal with whatever is happening without being burdened—or crippled—by our judgment of "what it means." *It* may not "mean" anything.

Sometimes, it simply is. Let It Be and deal with it as it is.

Breaking The Reaction Cycle

One thing that can prevent us from Letting It Be is getting caught up in reacting. We get triggered instead of calmly observing what is happening in the moment.

Many of us go through our entire lives "reacting" to our world and others in one of three ways:

1. **Denial.** This is the act of sticking our fingers in our ears, shutting our eyes, and going "La, la, la, la, la…" It's the decision to ignore something that may be very important. I had a close friend who ignored some serious health issues because she just didn't want to know. Her denial ended her life at 49 years old.

2. **Delusion.** Also known as lying to ourselves, this is the act of believing something that just is not factually accurate. My friend,

who passed away, deluded herself into believing that the lower back pain was just a mild kidney infection without getting the proper tests. Turns out she was suffering from heart failure. Back pain is a common symptom of cardiac disease in women.

3. **Fixing**. Actively attempting to control that which we have no control over is what we refer to in our coaching methodology as Fixing. It is the instant need to categorize everything as good or bad, right or wrong, when we don't have all of the facts. Our minds tend to take shortcuts and force everything we observe to fit into our worldview. This gives us a false sense of control when the real work of understanding has not occurred.

Learning to Let It Be can help us break out of these patterns. It will put us on a path to being able to Learn From It, Let It Go and Live Now.

> *The inspiration for the Beatles song "Let It Be" came when Paul McCartney said he had a dream about his mother during the tense period surrounding the "Get Back"/"Let It Be" recording sessions. McCartney explained that his mother—who died of cancer when he was fourteen—was the inspiration for the "Mother Mary" lyric. McCartney later said, "In the dream, she told him that everything would be okay and just to Let It Be. It was great visiting with her again."*

Let It Be is the first step to dealing effectively with adversity. It is the act of acceptance of life as it comes to us. It doesn't mean we have to like what's happening or approve of it. It means we must accept that it is happening and understand that it isn't a judgment. Bad things sometimes happen to good people. The power of Let It Be is to face reality without being paralyzed by worry or regret. Its effect is to pull us into the present moment, where we are free to regard what has happened with detachment and then say, "OK, what do I do about it?"

Some people believe that they can't do this because anything that happens to them must be a judgment from God. They make things *personal*.

"Hey!" I want to say to them, "Haven't good things happened to you, too? Does that mean that God can't decide whether you're a good person or a bad person?"

I prefer to believe that God has a much bigger plan than I will ever fully understand. Sometimes, things just happen, and all we can do is respond in the best way we know how.

The principle of Let It Be embodies what I believe to be one of the most fundamental truths about living:

Almost any event in life can yield blessings, even multiple blessings, provided that we respond to what is happening. Let me give you an example. A few years back, the wife of a man I know nearly died following a severe asthma attack. Fortunately, she recovered, but her husband, who had been terribly afraid of being left as a single father, experienced post-traumatic stress disorder (PTSD) starting several months after his wife's hospitalization. As part of his PTSD, he developed an obsession with death. So, in the wake of these twin traumas, my friend and his wife had a choice of how to respond.

They could have:

a) Chosen to see the events as "bad" and personal and retreated from life, never daring to take a hike in the mountains again because of the woman's asthma risk or living in terror of a recurrence of the man's PTSD.

b) Chosen to see the events as something that just happened and say, "OK, what can we take from these experiences that will make us better?"

I probably don't have to tell you that this couple chose Door #2. The woman got better treatment for her asthma and is symptom-free today. The man found out that the constant stress of his PTSD had contributed to high blood pressure, so he chose to lose 50 pounds and get into the best shape of his life. He also rejected his lifelong atheism and embraced a life of Christian faith. Together, they reversed their decision to stop at just one child and decided to have another. Having faced death, they opted to create more life. The woman gave birth to their second child and has since gotten in the best shape of her life, as well. So, from their deeply frightening trauma, they have transformed their lives by seeing the events as "something that happened." They could not change the events, but they could choose to use them as catalysts for positive change and growth. That is what Let It Be can do for you.

Exercise: Find the Blessing

In even the most traumatic events, there are usually hidden blessings if we choose to see them. What blessings can you find in your past disasters? This exercise can help you uncover them. If you'd like more room to write, download this sheet as a PDF from www.Lifeonomics.com.

Find the Blessing	
What happened?	What blessings came from it?

Worry is interest paid on trouble before it comes *due.*

—William Ralph *Inge*

Not Good, Not Bad

The heart and soul of Let It Be is facing the facts. It is accepting whatever is happening and recognizing what it truly is, without judgment or reading emotions into it. It's not our responsibility to make someone's behavior good or bad, right or wrong. We're only responsible for our own behavior unless we have children who are minors. So, with everyone else, we just love them and Let Them Be. We can accept the facts of a situation, even if we hate and despise them, and use them as rocket fuel to completely transform our lives without being attached to the situation anymore.

To make Let It Be work, we must become less "dualistic" in our thinking. Dualism means that we judge everything as being either good or bad. Forcing the label of good or bad on all things can be destructive when we're confronted with personal adversity.

It is far more productive to regard the things that happen to us as morally neutral. They simply are. Most often, "good" and "bad" are simply relative human constructs that we use to categorize things that are and are not in our short-term interest. But this immediate perspective can be deceptive and can blind us to important choices we may need to make. So, rather than judge things as good or bad, it is often wiser to set aside such judgments and focus on how we will respond.

Let's use personal finance as an example. You're 40 years old and suffer an unexpected setback in your business that eventually leads to bankruptcy, the loss of everything you've built, and starting over again in middle age.

Your big question is: "How do I respond?" Suppose you can see clearly, instead of beating yourself to death with regrets over past financial decisions. In this case, you can focus on paying your debts, create a new financial strategy, and end up living a simpler life that can be more financially secure—one where people, health, confidence and free time are more important than accumulating a massive portfolio of property. So, if by age

55, you are solvent, saving, and living a much more rewarding life than when you were 40 and swimming in debt, was your bankruptcy a good thing or a bad thing? It was both bad in the moment and good in the end. So why judge? It simply happened, and your response to it was productive and wise. For adults, nothing in life is purely good or purely bad, so why burden yourself with categories? See what it is clearly. That is, Let It Be, and then figure out your next move.

It's Not A Problem, It's A Challenge

How we describe something will constrain the ways we feel able to respond to it. This is why, if you participate at all in self-help culture and listen to motivational speakers like Tony Robbins, you'll rarely hear anyone call a problem a "problem." Instead, they call it a "challenge." This reframes the situation from something inherently negative to one that requires better choices and some fortitude, but can be overcome. There is a huge difference between the two perceptions. It's the difference between saying, "I am going through a bad time," and "I am bad." One is temporary and offers hope of change; the other is near-permanent or certainly a lot harder to change.

Let's say we've received a cancer diagnosis. Seen on a purely emotional level, that's an awful, horrible thing, right? But how you react to that news will determine the progress of your disease and possibly make the difference between living for another year or 20 more years. If you tell yourself (and everyone else) that you just received a "death sentence," you're probably going to take a fatalistic attitude toward your disease, become passive, sit back and hope for a miracle without taking any steps to heal yourself. So, labels do matter.

On the other hand, let's say we view cancer as a "challenge." We're more likely to adopt a fighting stance, start an anti-cancer diet, and begin working out and meditating—in short, doing everything we can to give ourselves the best chance of beating the disease. We're not going to sit back passively and depend on doctors alone. The late Randy Pausch, the professor with terminal cancer who wrote the bestselling *The Last Lecture*, is a stirring example of this kind of spirit.

We are not our thoughts. They come from us, but they are not US. Our thoughts are a symptom of our whole selves. All our lives, we exist within a self-generated storyline produced by our minds, the subjective experience of what it is like to be us. That's something unique to us, something that can't be validated or disproved by science; it just is. While that's remarkable, it also can be destructive if we cannot get out of that subjective state from time to time to see things as they are, not as our emotions tell us they must be.

When we Let It Be, we take away the power that any negative thoughts have over us because we separate ourselves from them. This is the power of objectivity. We are all blessed with the faculty of reason, and part of being a reasoning being is the ability to switch back and forth between the subjective inner life and the objective, just-the-facts-ma'am outer life, where judgments are obsolete. If we wish to enhance our future and live without worry and regret, developing this ability within our minds will help.

Stop Worrying About Others

In working to alter patterns of thinking and become more objective about the adversity of life, one of the greatest obstacles can be other people. Everyone seems to want to empathize with someone who is going through adversity, and that's admirable. It also may mean they are projecting their fears and anxieties onto you, acting as an echo chamber for your worries or regrets. Especially when the person is someone you care about or who influences your thinking (like a mentor or spiritual leader), this can amplify your inability to Let It Be. We're social beings, after all, and the mirror neurons in our brains make it inevitable that we reflect the behaviors and emotions of others back to them.

So, another crucial aspect of Let It Be is this: *Just because someone else drinks poison doesn't mean we have to get sick.*

In other words, when it comes to the behavior and feelings of other people, we can Let It Be, just as we do with our own. You are not responsible for how your mother responds to your miscarriage or how your best friend reacts to the news of your health problem. We cannot allow ourselves to be affected—or infected—by someone else's emotional response to our situation. We cannot change their response. It simply IS, and part of Let It Be is allowing other people's reactions to what happens to bounce off you like raindrops off the ground without letting it soak in and affect your own rational, non-dualistic analysis of the situation. We can accept that people cannot be other than who and what they are. This allows us to accept their concern for what it is—their way of expressing love and support—without labeling it as dysfunctional, negative, or anything else that devalues it.

Letting Go of Comparison

But let's step out of crisis mode now and think about the larger implications of this aspect of Let It Be. Most of the time, we're not going to be in crisis; we're going to be living our lives and doing what we do every day. However, like it or not, most of us are constantly comparing ourselves to other people and usually coming up short. We seem to be programmed to position ourselves next to the rich and the beautiful and assume that they are superior to us. As a result, we feel bad about ourselves. Someone who has never been married might envy a friend who has a wonderful spouse and children, while completely overlooking the blessings in their own life and missing out on their own joy. Why live this way?

Let It Be means that we stop comparing ourselves to others and also stop worrying about what others think of us. We have no idea what journey another person is going through. Social media posts and exterior facades reveal next to nothing. I have driven by magnificent homes in some of the wealthiest parts of the country and assumed that the people who live in them must be financially secure beyond my wildest dreams, only to see in the news a few months later that those same palatial homes were up for foreclosure sale. We cannot know what kind of life a person is living, what they think of us, or how meaningful their judgment of us would be if we knew it. So why worry about it? We Let It Be and live according to what seems right to us rather than imagining that some unseen social judge and jury are sitting in the next room deciding whether we're thin enough, rich enough, or cool enough.

I heard about a terrific example of this. A young mother was with her five-year-old son at a Chinese restaurant. The boy started pitching the mother of all temper tantrums. If you have kids, you've likely been in this position. Do you disrupt your meal? Bribe your child to be quiet and reinforce the behavior? Or let him scream himself to exhaustion as he becomes a pariah to the other diners?

To her credit, this young mother chose to let her son kick and scream on the floor until he was spent while the other diners stared, and she calmly ate her meal. Then, when he saw he was not going to get his way, the boy sat down meekly in his chair. But his mother wasn't done: she made him walk by himself to each table and apologize to the other guests for disrupting their lunch. That mom was one cool customer. She knew she was being judged by the other diners (bad mother, rude woman and so on), but she didn't let that concern her. She acted as she knew she must. In the end, I think she won everyone's admiration.

No man ever sank under the burden of the day.
It is when tomorrow's burden is added to the burden of today that the weight
is more than a man can bear.

—George MacDonald,
Scottish author, poet, and Christian minister

What Are You Obligated To Do?

We burden ourselves with many things that we believe we *must* do: social obligations, owning certain material things, voting for political candidates because our parents did and so on. Worrying about what could happen and fretting over what others think of us are parts of the weighty sense of *obligation* that makes us feel that we are always laboring, always bent double beneath the load of choices we did not make.

Yet, everything is a choice. We choose to saddle ourselves with obligation. It's just that after a while, we lose the sense that we've given ourselves any sort of extraordinary load to bear. It's like the old story of prospectors' mules who meet while tied up at a local saloon. One mule looks normal, but the other has its back bowed practically into a "U" shape by the massive amount of supplies and tools tied to it. Astonished by the other mule's ability to even move while so laden, the first mule says, "How do you manage that load?" The second mule replies, "What load?"

Exercise: Self-Imposed Obligations

We often imprison ourselves behind walls of the things we think we have no choice but to do. How have you trapped yourself behind self-imposed obligations? What can you do to escape? Download this self-test at www. Lifeonomics.com.

Self-Imposed Obligations			
What's my obligation?	Self-imposed? Y/N	How does it affect me?	What can I do about it?

Self-imposed obligation can be a prison. The self-imposed duty to "fix" someone or something can tie you to something that holds you back from your hopes and dreams. Let's say one of your parents becomes bitter and angry after the other dies. How much of your time and energy should you spend trying to "fix" your living parent and get him or her to see that life is still worth living? In my opinion, we can give them love and support, point them to some worthwhile books or a good therapist, and then let them make their own decisions. We have to live our own lives. We cannot control theirs, and it is not our duty to "fix" them, nor are we required to do penance for adversity or some long-ago sin or by being miserable along with our parent. If you assign yourself the duty of sharing the misery, you will only become miserable as well. Instead, the best we can do is to let go of that obligation and live in a way that inspires other people to follow our example. Otherwise, we have to Let It Be and Let Them Be.

What do our self-assigned obligations say about us? How have we burdened ourselves out of an unquestioned sense of duty? If you stepped back from those obligations and realized that they were not obligatory but optional, how might that change your life? Some obligations are mandatory: paying our debts, taking care of our young children, being faithful to our spouse, obeying the law. Those you either did not choose or chose and cannot reverse; in some cases, being a grownup means living with consequences. But how many of the so-called "things I must do" are burdens *we* have placed on our own backs? I suggest everyone take a long, hard look at that. If you are imprisoned by obligations that exist only in your mind, then it's time to realize that you can Let It Be in that area of your life as well. People walk around carrying the weight of all the things—i.e., responsibilities—that they believe they *should* be worried about. This becomes neurotic behavior. Learning to put down all this illusory responsibility can change your life.

Living At Arm's Length

In the end, I'm talking about the act of *detachment*, a concept that has its roots in many traditions of ancient wisdom. Keep in mind, I'm not talking about living without emotion and being detached from the people and pursuits that you care about. What I am talking about is keeping life's circumstances at arm's length, realizing that they reveal nothing about who or what you are. Some people feel that doing this is cruel. After all, aren't you supposed to cry with your friend when she tells you that she's failed to get pregnant or to get outraged for your buddy when he tells you that his son wrecked the car? That might seem the most empathetic thing to do, but how does sharing in someone else's emotional drama help them? Yes, it might give them a momentary boost, and there's nothing wrong with doing that. However, you can quickly detach from the other person's emotional flow and instead focus your energies on the one thing you can do for someone facing adversity: *give them the support they need to respond in the most positive and productive way possible.*

From this perspective, not attaching to things or people becomes an act of compassion for yourself and others. Let me repeat: this does *not* mean becoming emotionally distant. It means refraining from instantly judging anything as good or bad and, therefore, not attaching meaning to it so you don't trigger emotional reactions that rob you of your ability to deal with what is and what must be done. The objectivity of the physician, the attorney, the wealth advisor, and the therapist is all necessary because most of us cannot get past our habit of attaching personal importance and meaning to the things that happen to us. But when you can do this, worry and regret quickly become things of the past.

As you begin your exploration of the L Steps toolkit, work on developing your "mindfulness," that is, your awareness of how your habits of thought affect your progress throughout your day. Thoughts are habits, and changing them requires training and practice. Starting now, spend 30 days practicing being mindful of what is in front of you and whether or not you are Letting It Be. Look at the facts without emotion, whether the event is an argument with your spouse or the fact that you did not go to the gym this morning. Divorce yourself from the meaning behind the event and what it might say about you.

Look only at the facts of what happened. Now, how can you best respond? What result would you like your response to produce?

I suggest even posting Let It Be notes around your home or workspace as reminders. You'll need a reminder to stand back, be mindful of your thought process, and Let It Be. This new habit may not come easily at first. It can be hard to form new habits. But as you do this more and more often, you will see that what is happening to you is not your identity. Things happen and have only the meaning we ascribe to them, no more, no less. Whether what's happening is a bear market or a relationship problem, detaching yourself from its meaning and turning your attention to your response frees you to concentrate on today instead of worrying about tomorrow or regretting what you did yesterday to create the situation. You become centered in the "challenge of now" and learn to put your energies and passions to work, creating the best outcome possible.

That's the first of our L Steps. In the next chapter, we're going to look at the steps that make that positive outcome a reality—the Systems, Strategies and Structures that will transform your life.

Summary

- Let It Be means accepting events as they happen without judgment.
- It also means letting people be who they are without trying to control them.
- Any life event can provide blessings depending on our attitude.
- Dualistic thinking divides everything into Good and Bad.
- We are not our thoughts.
- We are not responsible for the actions or choices of others.
- Detachment means not attaching meaning or self-definition to events.

To-Do List

- Stop taking responsibility for the actions of people in our lives.
- Train ourselves to quit judging events as Good and Bad, but just see them as Being.
- Recall a difficult life event and find at least three blessings that came from it.
- Post "Let It Be" reminders around our home and workspace.

CHAPTER SIX:

Learn From It

"If we knew what we were doing, it would not be called research, would it?"

– Albert Einstein

I had just come home from a session with my trainer at the gym, wearing my T-shirt and shorts, when I started noticing that some of the doors were open and a big jar of change in the kitchen was gone. It was only 10:30 in the morning, so my first reaction was to call Joy. Was she upset about something? Had she needed gas money?

I was walking through the house, doing the "Baby, are you okay?" thing on my call to her, when I rounded a corner and saw a shadow in the next room. Out of the corner of my eye, I saw someone start to run. Now, I'd been trained for years to be the security on our farm with my brother. My father was a railroad engineer who was away a lot of the time. My brother Joel was a military chief of police and SWAT team commander. I'm the guy you always want to have in an emergency… well, most of the time.

As Mike Tyson says, everyone has a plan until they get punched in the face. And instead of doing any of the things I was trained to do, I lost it. I started chasing him and screaming at him. I chased him right through the glass door, which he had broken to gain entry, with jagged glass still jutting out around the edges. There was a voice coming out of me, I call the Evil Rob voice. I won't go into all of the things that Evil Rob was yelling, but let's just say the threat of violence may have been involved.

As I chased the intruder onto the front lawn of my neighbor, I could see he was around 20 years old, and he had my Oakley backpack on. He'd dumped all the change in it, and it had my laptop in it. He had my stepson's Xbox in one hand and controllers in the other, and he was trying to run from me with all that stuff. We got about halfway through the neighbor's yard when I asked myself what I was going to do if I caught him. We were going to be on one of the busiest corners of West Little Rock, with traffic everywhere. Did I really want to catch this young man and… what…beat him up?

So, I stopped and, with all the force and fury I could muster, yelled, "Drop my stuff!!" Okay, I didn't say "stuff," but you get the picture. And to my complete surprise, he did. He dropped everything on my neighbor's front lawn and kept running. I stopped, grabbed my stuff, and called 911. The young man apparently lived one block away in an apartment complex. One of the police cars that responded to my 911 call happened to be driving through the parking lot and recognized him by my description. He still, apparently, had some of our stuff in his pockets. They arrested him. It turned out he was a serial burglar. He was stealing people's stuff to pay for his drug problem.

By the time the police came to my house to interview me, Joy came screeching up her driveway in her Genesis. She'd driven 100 miles per hour from North Little Rock. I had forgotten to disconnect the phone, so she'd heard me screaming at the guy the whole time and, of course, was coming to save me… all five-foot-one-inches of her.

The experience was traumatic for both of us. Joy had never felt safe in the house alone, and this violation made it much worse.

It was easy to come up with a conclusion like "The world is an unsafe place" and decide we had to move in case something like this happened again, but we decided to Let it Be and Learn From It. I didn't want to sell our house and move because of a petty crime. So, instead, we bought a new alarm system and put in sensors that made it a lot better. Although we already had the older alarm system, we had never actually used it before, so we committed to integrating this one into our daily lives. To this day, when I open the garage door or close it, I turn on the alarm using the key fob from the new system. We have video cameras everywhere, and Joy has a key fob beside our bed to turn the alarm on and off. We had to not only upgrade the system but also incorporate it into our lives in a meaningful way, which took some training and practice. Only after we updated the alarm and then took the time, energy and focus to integrate it did we fully learn from the experience.

Letting It Be will only help us benefit from an experience if we Learn From It without judging it *and* change our Thoughts, Words and Actions in response. (Check out Exercise 10 in the Appendix if you want to get better at developing this awareness.) Some people experience this kind of change overnight because of a life-changing event, like a near-death experience, but generally, change is hard. To make real changes in our lives, we usually have to invest the time, attention, and energy to reprogram ourselves. Most of us need to put Systems, Strategies and Structures into place, like the alarm system in my home or possibly something much bigger. Maybe join a life coaching group at our coaching practice, where we bring together people with similar goals.

Not everything we learn warrants change. Sometimes, experiencing it is enough. Maybe it broadens our palate. So it is important to ask ourselves a question, "Is it Truly Important enough to me to change?" It's okay to decide we don't want to change, or the time isn't right to do so. But if we want to change, it will require an investment of time, energy, focus and sometimes money to put Systems, Strategies and Structures in place to support us.

Systems, Strategies and Structures

Quick: Where do you keep the salt and pepper in your home? If you're like most people, you'll say something along the lines of "There's a cabinet in the kitchen, and inside of it, there's a spot where the salt and pepper go."

At the most basic level, where you keep the salt and pepper is a *system*: one you probably seldom think about. If you bring the shakers into another room and they never make it back to the kitchen, your system will break down and you may end up hunting for them when you planned to do something else… wasting time, energy and focus. That's probably why the old homemaker's adage, "A place for everything, and everything in its place," is so valuable. If you don't have a place for something, it may be time to create one, build another closet, or donate it. My dad was a fanatic about this when it came to tools. If we had a tool, but I didn't put it back where it was supposed to be, we might as well not have the tool.

This is true of experiences, as well. If we have an experience and mentally file it in a place where we can Learn From It, we can tap into it when we need to, and it becomes useful to us. However, we need to document and store these experiences in a consistent place—a journal, a recipe file, an app on our phone—just like our things, or we often won't be able to recall them. If it doesn't have a home where we can find it, we won't be able to use it. We may be able to call that knowledge back up here and there, but in many cases, the chance we will do that is slim to none. This is one area where the right tools can make all the difference.

Where you keep your salt and pepper shakers, tools, and experiences are small examples of how, in almost every area of our lives, there are systems, processes and routines we follow. They feed into the larger system of our lives. We often do the same thing over and over again without recognizing this.

The question is: Did we design them? Did they just happen to us? Or did we inherit them? And most importantly, are they serving us?

Most of us don't give these questions much thought. However, bringing consciousness to the routines of our daily lives and deciding whether we want to continue them or refine them can unlock tremendous power to learn from them, change how we spend our time and attention, and become fully engaged in each moment and activity. Change of any kind is not going to be easy at first, and it takes conscious, deliberate thought and integration. One of the most powerful transformation tools for me in my life has been our *Lifeonomics* Coaching app. Using the app to create, store and access new routines has changed my life dramatically, and I think it could change yours too. You can find the app on our website, www.Lifeonomics.com.

Our coaching program is designed to help people wake up and realize they actually have an attention—and then convert that attention to intention. Very early in our coaching programs, we ask questions like, "What does health look like to you?" By having people write down what their values and goals are, we're trying to create intention. Attention flows to intention. In order to create transformation, we have to then bring integration.

Intention, in its highest form, is our vision. It is a plan. How do we bring that vision out of our conscious minds and into our lives? We have to incorporate our intention into our Systems, Strategies and Structures until we can integrate those Systems, Strategies and Structures into who we are. practice something enough, learn and listen to something frequently, associate with others on the same path and experience social contagion, we will see change. It takes time for us to retrain our subconscious. It's not supposed to be easy to reprogram automated systems. If it were, life would be very frustrating. Imagine having a five-minute exposure to something that completely reprogrammed a habit like driving.

In setting an intention, we have to focus on the mundane systems in life. It helps to look at our lives like a movie, in which the day unfolds in scenes. That might start with asking, "What is scene one?" Scene one could be the moment you wake up and your morning routine. In essence, you have a script for it. I heard a member of SEAL Team 6 give a keynote once. He shared a saying that is fully integrated into their training and missions. "Slow is smooth. Smooth is fast." That one saying has had a massive impact on our coaching methodology. I now look at everything through the lens of "How smooth can I make each scene of my life?"

In a movie, where everyone is supposed to be standing in a certain spot, there's a process called blocking, where we map out where everyone stands. That way, we don't have to do multiple takes of the same scene.

We can do the same thing in our personal lives, where we set the stage the night before so we don't have distractions or obstacles. Everything is smooth. In my own life, I go to sleep in a set of warmups with my hoodie and hat hanging on the bedpost. When I wake up, I move into my meditation right away using a routine on our coaching app I wrote for myself called "Mind & Spirit Practice." I have 15 minutes up to about 45 minutes of meditation and then transition into 15 minutes of prayer, scripture reading and affirmations. That routine ends. Next, I get right into my Jeep and drive to the gym for my strength training routines and other exercises or load up my bike for a 15-20 mile ride on the beautiful Arkansas River Trail. Over time, these morning routines have helped me fall in love with my mornings and live powerfully in the moment.

It's what I call setting the stage for my day—a concept that goes back to my experience in live productions. We don't want to be setting the stage when we're also trying to perform. If we take a routine like this and completely internalize it, it becomes a *structure*. This helps us stay on course during the day. Our brain treats routines like rituals. Our brains use minor rituals to shift gears. So, when I turn on the lights in the morning and start my routine, it signals to my brain that I'm entering the moving part of the day. If I don't have that ritual, that doesn't happen. This is part of my overall *strategy* for having a productive day.

Putting this system in place is better than beating myself up for not being one of those people who just get out of bed and meditate or go running. There's no reason for me to be that person. What I need is a plan of action that will work for me, one day at a time.

Once we have a smooth routine, it can then evolve. We create the movie of our lives, and the scenes become our history. That history brings wisdom.

Staying focused on what we can control

Keep in mind that as we've discussed, we can only affect what we have control over—our own Thoughts, Words and Actions, our perspectives and attitudes. Consciously focusing on things we can control—and not on what everyone else needs to change—can enable us to slow down and experience life to the fullest.

Putting Systems, Strategies and Structures in place can help us stay focused on what we can control. Remember the days when it was easy to forget our bank card at an ATM? Now, that's all but impossible because most banks use systems where we can't get our money out of the machine without retrieving our cards first.

As we go through the L Steps, we ultimately want to bring consciousness to the routines in our daily lives so we can fine-tune them if need be. Most of us have processes in our lives for almost everything we do—deciding what to have for dinner, washing dishes, you name it. We often do the same thing over and over again without recognizing this. Once we become conscious of this, we may need to add routines and other systems that help us change how we spend our time or our focus—activities that, if we keep doing them, make all other things easier. It's about prioritizing things that are going to have the highest impact. If we're not achieving our goals, it may come down to our routines. Which routines are we observing? Which ones have fallen away? Are there any routines we need to add to help us stay on track?

Sometimes, we need our systems to act as barriers against things that will derail us. If you are overcoming an addiction, for instance, you may need to change the people you associate with to stay sober. Similarly, in areas of your life where it's hard for you to stay disciplined, you may need to put into place a system where you routinely *seek counsel* to prevent you from making mistakes.

A wealth advisor can be part of a system like this. You've probably heard about incremental and exponential growth. Sometimes, there's the opposite. We can have incremental deterioration or exponential destruction. I see this all the time in my wealth management practice. Reasonably normal people with very little financial wealth inherit a large sum of money, and it ultimately destroys their lives. It causes so much stress and pressure, so that all they want to do is spend it quickly, so their life They feel they have no choice but to give it away. In some cases, they develop addictions.

An alternative to this might be to take a little vacation, give the windfall to their wealth advisor to manage, and have the money work for them. This can help protect them from greedy relatives or a new boyfriend who wants to borrow $100,000. They can say, "I have to run this past my wealth advisor. If he says it's okay, then I'll consider it." As you might have guessed, I often say, "That sounds like a terrible financial decision based on your plan and goals." They go back and say, "Nope, sorry—I can't do it." That protects the relationship for the client and leaves them with some financial security.

Seeking counsel in this way is a form of delegation. You're outsourcing the knowledge and wisdom for this particular thing to someone else because you're not willing to put in the time and energy into becoming an expert in this field, or because it serves you best to have a third party shielding you from conflict with your loved ones and friends.

Once we put Systems, Strategies and Structures in place, if something goes wrong, there's an opportunity to ask, "What happened here—and how can we keep that one thing from happening again by changing our system?" It's almost always a conversation about process, not people. If the process is strong enough, and something goes wrong anyway, it is often because people failed to implement that process.

Putting systems in place prevents us from having to make the same decisions over and over again. If you've hired a wealth management team, you probably get together to make decisions twice a year. That prevents decision fatigue, so you have the energy you need to make big decisions when they come up. Putting security cameras around the perimeter of your property can work the same way. You can set them and forget them as long as you periodically assess and adjust the system to make sure it's working.

Often, we need to bring more organization to our lives to see things clearly. In areas of my life where I seem to keep doing the same things over and over, and I don't grow, often it has to do with a lack of organization as much as anything. Any time invested in keeping things in order generally pays for itself. We can have the best tools in the world, but a tool is not a tool unless we know where to get it when we need it and how to use it.

Sustainable change requires that we alter our Systems, Strategies and Structures, like avoiding triggers by modifying our routines. Conscious decisions and accountability strengthen new behaviors over time.

Defining Systems, Strategies and Structures

Before we discuss how to put the right Systems, Strategies and Structure in place, let's get clear on what we mean within our methodology when we use these phrases, so we have a common language.

Systems are organized ways of doing things that we put to work for ourselves on a regular basis. Sometimes, we create them ourselves, as we do in our kitchens and tool sheds. Other times, they're created by someone else or an institution like the government or a big company.

It doesn't matter as much who created the systems we use, but rather that we use the ones that serve our higher purpose. What happens to many people, though, is that instead of creating a process that reflects them or tailoring an existing one, they use hand-me-down processes from others. As Don Miguel Ruiz said, we get "domesticated by other people," and often, these processes don't work well for them at all or need some customization.

Being conscious of the systems we use and taking ownership of them prevents us from having to make the same decisions over and over again and allows us to design our own life experiences. It prevents decision fatigue, so we have mental space for other things.

Keep in mind that processes need to be repeated regularly to help us. A financial plan alone won't help us. We need a financial planning process that we can return to if something changes. If we're not adjusting it and revamping it when needed, it's not worth anything. A plan is just a map before the journey. It provides us with some understanding of when we're on track or off track as we live our lives, but if there isn't a process to adjust it as we go, it won't be of much help.

Sometimes, we need our systems to act as barriers against things that will derail us. For instance, starting a regular meditation practice can help us train our minds to recognize any patterns of thinking, like delusion and denial, that keep us stuck in the same old feedback loops and patterns of thinking and behavior.

Strategies are decisions we've made in advance to embrace a particular approach to something. They're similar to tactics and techniques, except that they're predetermined decisions to do things a certain way. You might never need to use these strategies—like one for surviving a bear attack—but by nailing them down, we can free ourselves from making things up as we go along, something we may not have the luxury of doing in the moment.

One strategy you might rely on regularly is an investment strategy. You and your wealth advisor may have decided that you'll include certain types of investments in your portfolio and exclude others.

Like systems, strategies are only valuable when you use them. For instance, maybe you've set a goal of eating healthier for the coming year. Your strategy for taking care of your health might involve embracing exercise and a healthy diet under your doctor's care rather than going on medication. That is a strategy—provided you commit to it by scheduling supporting actions, like gym workouts, time for meal planning, and cooking in blocks on your calendar. If it's not on your calendar, you're giving in to the 3Ds—Delusion, Denial and Distraction—and it's likely to fall by the wayside, like most New Year's resolutions. The 3Ds are why people don't change. Strategies like time blocking are why they do.

You may also have strategies for dealing with other people. I have a strategy I use for communicating with people in my life who have given me input or feedback: React, Respond, or Refrain. I don't use this strategy all the time, but I know how I will respond when certain scenarios come up, and it's super helpful to remember that in almost every case, we don't actually owe any response at all to other people. We can simply Refrain and walk away.

Structures are often physical environments and barriers that ensure success. For instance, if you're changing your diet to make it healthier, you might join a local food coop that delivers fresh fruits and vegetables to your family every week or two. That increases the odds you'll have them in the house and eat these foods, not chips and ice cream. You don't have to go to the store or choose the fresh produce. It just shows up. You have to cook it, or it goes bad.

If you take a system and completely internalize it, it becomes a structure. A simple example is a calendar. If you want to get more done, stop and plan. I use time-blocking on my Outlook calendar to reduce decision fatigue and stress, stay fully present and maximize productivity. That includes transition periods between tasks. At least 30 minutes a day go into handling my schedule, making changes and re-blocking. In doing so, I am deciding if something is Truly Important to me.

There are several reasons to do this. First, it brings accountability. I know exactly what I'm supposed to be doing right now and if I'm actually doing it. The absence of accountability contributes significantly to the chaos in our lives. One example is the road construction in front of my house, which has been ongoing for the past two years. It is wide enough for two lanes and a turning lane, but for a while during construction, there were no lines in the road on the newly paved road, and there was no median. When they finally put in a median, it was hard to see after dark. There were still no lines. One night, I heard a loud crash and went running outside. Someone had hit the median, set off both of his airbags and flattened two tires. Fortunately, he was okay, but we quickly called the road contractor to let him know. He put in reflectors to show the median was there, and later the lines were painted.

Life is similar to a road in this count: Without structures like lines and reflectors, it's hard to know when we're moving out of our lane. With the right structures, we can notice we're getting distracted by something else, even if it's our own obsessing, and refocus.

The right structures give us presence. If we're driving and try to listen to a podcast during that time, we may be less focused. At the same time, we don't want to drive with tunnel vision. We need to pay attention to what's going on around us. To that end, the next time you're driving, try doing nothing but drive and pay attention to your five senses. Ask yourself: What am I seeing? What do I smell around me? What am I hearing? How does the engine sound? How does the seat feel? Etc. Just observe without judging. It can not only make you more mindful but also make you a better driver.

I discovered this while renting a new Audi on vacation. It was a cool car with different controls inside, to the extent that I could barely drive it. I had to pay attention to it in a way I don't with my Jeep. In my Jeep, I experience what's called hypnotic adaptation. We get used to things to the extent that we don't notice or savor them. There was so much change in my systems driving the Audi that it made me super-present.

Living in this way also helps my productivity. Switching between activities has a cost in terms of lost focus, so I've found it's best to design my days with fewer transitions. When I put something on my calendar, I know for a fact that I'm going to have the time to do the things I commit to doing. And if someone says, "Hey, can you do this tomorrow or the next day, I can look and see that there's no time unless I do it in the evening, as there is no time to squeeze it in during the day. White space is what we call the gaps or unblocked time. So, for instance, if I'm planning a band rehearsal with my bandmates, and there's going to be a bad storm, I'll move our band rehearsal to Saturday night, which is often white space for me, provided it works for everyone else, as well.

There is a metaphysical concept on the laws of prosperity that says the universe can't fill a space that's already occupied. That means if your glass is already full of something, it can't be filled up with something else. So, if you want a relationship, where is that space going to be? Relationships require an investment of time and attention. If there's no blocked time to build and deepen relationships, then that might be the first place to start. White space is available time, but there's another part of the concept of making space that we sometimes don't pay enough attention to, which is straight-out energy or bandwidth.

The result of paying attention is making choices that will let us live life more vividly and meaningfully. If I'm overdue to review several videos for my life coaching practice that are on a task list on my iPad and to provide feedback to my producer, but getting caught up this weekend will mean missing time going to a basketball game with my granddaughters, I have to choose which I'll sacrifice. And given how precious time with my granddaughters is, I may well opt to stick with our plan to go to the basketball game and fit the video review into another block of time—even if that means being overdue for one more week.

Beyond time blocking, I spent a lot of time organizing—one of the most powerful things we can do in our lives to make things smooth. If it isn't useful and doesn't bring you joy, donate it. Most of us have only so much closet space. Making a seemingly simple physical change in your life can bring needed structure that supports you in your life's goals.

Putting Systems, Strategies and Structures to work for you

Our Systems, Strategies, and Structures can be a powerful route to success in **Living Life,**[2] which is our way, in *Lifeonomics*, of creating a more meaningful, productive and exponentially satisfying existence. If we spend our whole day paying attention and being present, it's as if we are constantly in meditation from the time we wake up. The meditation starts in the morning, but it never really stops. After that, the way we move through reality is almost holographic. There's a little world that's happening around me, but it's just my perspective of it, as much as anything else, because I'm only seeing a fraction of it. That's the whole point—to let go of the past and future and all of the other baggage we carry around long enough to fundamentally experience our lives, moment by moment. It is our life to savor. If someone has been suffering for a long time, one moment of being free of pain and sickness would be priceless, but when we feel fine, we often take it for granted.

One way I stay connected with this truth is during my morning meditation. I do a gratitude exercise. I do a body scan, which is a form of meditation. I pay attention to my hands. I pay attention to my feet. And so on, until I cover each body part. And then I say to myself, "Wow. Nothing hurts. Everything works." I breathe and say, "I'm not in pain. I'm not nauseated. I seem to be thinking clearly, as far as I can tell. Right now, I'm blessed beyond measure."

There are many opportunities to practice this type of gratitude. If you love good food, you're probably aware that you can ruin a good meal and miss the whole experience of it if you rush through it. The next time you're sitting down to dinner, make it a point to slow down and savor it and see how different the experience can be.

I try to do this when I'm in my home office, as well. While I'm seated at my desk, I may be placing trades on millions of dollars for my clients. I might talk with several clients about their finances. But if I take some time between activities to look up and out my French doors, I'll notice that the red birds are flying around outside and talking to each other. And a hawk is swooping down to hunt a squirrel. That brings everything into balance. It feels effortless and graceful. And smooth. But if I get rushed into something else, my day starts to feel turbulent, like an airplane flying through a windstorm. I start to enter survival mode. I don't want turbulence. I want life to be slow and smooth. If I just do one thing now, without rushing, and do it well, I'll be lost in the right now and then in the next. That's flow, one of the highest states we can be in.

One of my coaches would remind me of how rare it is to be conscious of what we're doing, let alone in a flow state, by asking questions:

- What did you have for breakfast?
- What do you remember about yesterday?
- What do you remember about last week?

The point is that the things we don't remember are the things we probably didn't truly show up for—and we're only truly present about 10% of the time. As you start to apply Systems, Strategies and Structures, you'll create more opportunities to be truly present and experience flow.

Keep in mind, this is a work in progress. The idea is to build Systems, Strategies and Structures and put them under stress. Maybe I will try booking 20% more appointments next week. What is the weakest link in the system? Where do we need a fallback? If you've ever lost a critical piece of technology like your laptop or phone, you know how important it is to have systems in place for locating it, like a "find my device" app, and for backing it up.

The same holds true for the rest of our lives. I travel a lot, so I have an entirely separate set of clothes and personal care items for when I am on the road. It not only simplifies packing, but if my bag gets lost, I still have what I need when I get back home. Even so, I keep an AirTag in my backpack because losing it would be so inconvenient. I also keep duplicates of critical tools. I have three iPads and two laptops, for instance. I need these to keep going, so if one gets lost or fails, I still have access to another one. It's worth it to have some redundancy.

Once you've identified the critical tools or points in your own life, put systems in place to protect them. It takes time to put these systems in place, but it can save us days of frustration in the long run. Take inventory today: What are the five things that—if they go wrong, break down, disappear, or get stolen—will shut down my life today? Use time blocking to make time for this plan and process review. Keep in mind that it's a *process* to *review* your processes, and you may need to do this with someone else in a meeting to ensure it happens.

I do this with my wealth planning clients, having them come in to talk with me and my team every six months to make sure everything we put in place is still working for them and, if not, to course correct. Whether you're doing this alone or with a partner, ask yourself what you need to start doing, stop doing and/or keep doing. If something breaks in a big way, ask yourself if you need to throw out a whole system and start all over again. Sometimes, the breakdown comes in not using something. If you're not using it, and if it's not effective, efficient and easy for you, then what good is it? The whole point is to focus on things that matter to you, and if something is not easy, it will distract you from doing that.

Don't beat yourself up if a system breaks. Treat it as an opportunity to Learn From It. We don't want the door to fly off the jet at 10,000 feet. The same holds for your critical systems. If a system breaks, fine-tune or replace it. It's all about "engage" and then "adjust." Engage and adjust again. The idea that it's bad, somehow, if the system breaks down or something is wrong with the system misses the entire point of even using a system. Omani Carson, founder and chairman of Carson Group, has famously said thousands of times, "If it ain't broke, break it!" It's the best way to identify the weak points in any system.

So, how do you start applying them to your life today? We recommend taking inventory of the areas that bring you intrinsic wealth, such as work, relationships and spiritual life, and choose one or two where there are opportunities to bring positive change in your life. For instance, we all need deeply meaningful relationships where we feel truly seen and supported, but many people don't have them and struggle with loneliness. One reason is that to build these relationships, we need to be fully present and authentically care for others without judgment. That requires compassionate human connections, which take time to develop—something that can be done by planning activities with our loved ones and friends and blocking time on our calendar for it. The conscious application of systems to your time will allow you to spend more of it with the people who matter most to you, reduce resistance and maximize gratitude, growth and service of your higher purpose. That will allow you to make space for better relationships and live life as profoundly as possible.

As you put systems in place to make improvements in your life and build new skills, it's important to break them down step by step, the same way you might if you were teaching someone to drive a car—to essentially create Standard Operating Procedures for your life. When someone first gets behind the wheel, they don't know what they don't know, and they're what is called *unconsciously incompetent*. As they get better at driving, they may realize their mistakes and become *consciously incompetent*.

With more practice, they become *consciously competent* as they learn to drive effectively, but still have to really focus. And finally, as they master driving, they become *unconsciously competent*—both good at it and confident in their abilities—and their skill becomes automatic. You can only reach *unconscious competence* in any area of your life if you know the steps to master.

This can apply to both the big picture and practical, everyday matters that might otherwise distract you from the big picture. If, say, we've spent the time and energy to figure out the best process for changing the air filters in our house, why wouldn't we record that and then just stick with it as a standard operating procedure for life? It takes time to develop a process for something as simple as this, starting with knowing where the air filters are kept, having a step stool handy to reach them, and having a screwdriver ready. If we have to start from square one every time, it will take twice as long. If we're paying attention, we'll understand how dramatic an improvement we can see in our lives if we smooth out these systems and start recording them. Although it might seem tedious to document things like this, ChatGPT and AI are making it easier, and no doubt will continue to do so. Along the way, there will be many opportunities to make tweaks. Someone will show us a new way of doing something, and we'll say, "Holy cow, that's going to save me a lot of time and energy!" By continually updating our systems, we can bring smoothness to the scenes of our lives that have yet to

If there is a lot of room for improvement in your life, you may not be able to decide where to get started, so I'll make a suggestion: One of the most important systems you can put into place is a morning routine. I know exactly the order in which I do the things that are part of my mind and spirit routine, and I know they take 30-60 minutes. And if I do them in the wrong order, they won't work as well. As I write these words, I've meditated for more than 300 days out of the last 360. Using guided meditations has been life-changing for me, helping me to be present, set intentions, start the day with purpose, and feel gratitude. I use our *Lifeonomics* Coaching app, powered by LightBridge, which includes meditation, scripture, a purpose statement reading and tapping to guide me. Beyond this, I personally find that "eco-meditation," developed by Dawson Church and based on neuroscience, is particularly helpful, but there are many approaches that can work. My favorite of his books is "Bliss Brain." I use the guided meditations included in the audiobook 3-5 times per week.

Activities like these may be a natural part of some people's morning routine, but they aren't the first thing I think of doing on my own. Having a plan of action that will work for me, one day at a time, helps me accomplish what matters to me. Consistent meditation has tangible benefits, like slowing down time so you don't end up rushing and making mistakes. It can help keep us in a state of abundance and certainly improve our overall health. I'd rather put systems in place to ensure I do it than waste time regretting that I did not.

Exercise: Learn To Meditate

The most common remark about meditation is, "I've tried to meditate, and I can't." There's a simple reason for this: Most people try to start with difficult meditations before they learn the simple techniques. Instead, try these. If you want to carry this list with you, download it from www.Lifeonomics.com or use our coaching app and access the meditation routines there.

<table>
<tr><td align="center">Learn to Meditate</td></tr>
<tr><td>1. Gratitude Meditation – Make a short list of some of the things that you are most grateful for. Sit quietly somewhere that you will not be interrupted. Read each one and take a moment to feel the gratitude well up for each one. Just turning your attention to something you are grateful for can turn a moment of stress, say a traffic jam, into a moment of serenity</td></tr>
<tr><td>2. Pray and Wait Meditation – Almost every wisdom tradition or religion recommends some form of prayer and meditation. If prayer is part of your belief system, I recommend devoting a few minutes to praying every day. Make the prayer one of gratitude for all that you have and wish to have. Then wait. Expect nothing. Just wait for at least 60 seconds. If you have enough faith to believe in prayer, it makes sense to believe that on at least some level, it's a two-way conversation.</td></tr>
<tr><td>3. Sticky Note Meditation – This is my favorite beginning meditation. Sit somewhere quiet. Set a timer for one minute at first, working up to five minutes over time. Sit up straight and close your eyes. Do not TRY to stop thinking. Simply identify each thought as it pops up and imagine yourself putting a sticky note on it that says, "Thought." After some practice, it will become clear that you are not your thoughts. This is a first step toward bringing your mind and your thoughts under your control instead of the other way around.</td></tr>
<tr><td>4. Breath Meditation – Turn your attention to following the air as it moves in and out of your lungs. Breathe slowly and deeply. If you have a hard time holding your attention on your breathing, simply think these words as you breathe: "I am breathing in. I am breathing out." Another simple exercise is to breathe in for four seconds, hold for two, breathe out two seconds, then hold again, and so on.</td></tr>
</table>

Ultimately, what we want to do as we put Systems, Strategies and Structures in place is to bring consciousness to the routines in our daily lives so we can fine-tune them as we look to live in greater alignment with our goals. Learning from the past and planning for the future allows you to live fully in the present moment. Attachments to outcomes can be released if time is spent planning.

Systems, Strategies and Structures are one of the most powerful ways to help you Learn from It by allowing you the space to integrate new knowledge. We all need knowledge, wisdom and understanding to get through life. Knowledge is simply information. The application of that information is wisdom. Understanding is the third level. This is the idea that I truly understand how something works. Systems, Strategies and

Structures can help you reach a state of understanding so you not only know how to Live Life[2] and reach your most important goals, but you can also truly appreciate each day.

CHAPTER SEVEN:

Let It Go

"Peace is its own reward."

—Mahatma Gandhi

My brother Joel was a civilian chief of police in the Department of the Army. In 2019, he accepted an offer to become the Director of Operations at Kandahar Airfield in Afghanistan. It was a perfect assignment for him and gave him the ability to powerfully support the US Army war effort. This was his second trip to a combat zone. His first was as a U.S. Army infantry sergeant during Operation Desert Storm.

Joel was a born warrior from the time he was six or seven years old. He had an army outfit with toy guns and would come belly-crawling out of his room and disappear into the woods. He is consummate leader, and that job opportunity was an incredible calling for him.

Only a few months after he took his position, he became very sick. The military doctor called him in and said he had to go home.

"I've been serving my country continuously since I was 17 years old, and I have never *not* completed a mission," my brother said. "It's not starting now. You'll have to figure something out."

"You don't understand," the doctor told him. "If we don't send you home, you're going to die."

The doctor told Joel he had cancer, which turned out to be stage four lymphoma, which we have since learned was brought on by exposure to carcinogens during a weapons disposal operation in Desert Storm.

"Well, I guess you should've led with that," Joel replied with a smile.

Joel had to go home and endure a devastating round of chemo during the COVID-19 pandemic. That meant isolating himself for months while his immune system was compromised. He and his devoted wife, Amber, who stood by him, took care of him and ran the household through the entire ordeal, were dedicated to Joel getting better.

Although he regretted that he would never get to go on an assignment like that one again—Afghanistan fell soon after his departure—he realized there wasn't any point in dwelling on it. So, he Let It Go and moved on, realizing that dwelling on the past would hinder his growth. He turned his attention to beating cancer, and he and Amber have faced every challenge it has brought with faith and courage.

That's what Let It Go means: accept what has happened, Learn From It, and then drop it. Don't totally forget about it, but don't keep living in the past, either. Letting things go is extremely important because only then do you free your mind to start applying what you learned from your experience. By learning from experience yet releasing its hold, we can apply new insights.

"We cannot solve our problems with the same thinking we used when we created them."

—Albert Einstein

When we cling to adversity—or more specifically, go on beating ourselves up for something we did wrong—we spend all our time blaming ourselves or others, feeling guilty and not applying the lessons we've learned. We only have so much time, attention and energy in the day, so if we exhaust them by wallowing in regret and guilt, we've got nothing left to allow us to change our behavior and make better decisions.Our tank is empty.

Let It Go means owning the fact that, although we might not like what's happened, we can take new knowledge from it and then get to work on becoming a wiser, better person as a result of it. It is making a conscious effort to turn away from it, as we learned in the chapter on Let It Be. If we're going to be mentally healthy and happy, we have no other choice. We can just say, "I've taken everything of value that I can out of this experience, and there's no value in obsessing over it. I'm going to accept it, and Let It Go."

"The sun shines and warms and lights us and we have no curiosity to know why this is so; but we ask the reason of all evil, of pain and hunger, and mosquitoes and silly people."

—*Ralph Waldo Emerson*

A "No-Why Zone"

When I tell people that **Lifeonomics** is about not being attached to life, a lot of them look at me strangely, as though I've just said that the philosophy is about leaving their spouse and not caring about anything. That is not what Let It Go is about at all. Let It Go is accepting what happened while learning from the experience and shifting our focus forward. It is grabbing one's ears and choosing to focus elsewhere for now. We don't have to make what we are turning away from bad or wrong. We don't even have to necessarily work through it. That process of shifting focus is letting go, to some degree, of whatever it was that we were focused on. If we just change our Thoughts, Words and Actions and shift our focus, we'll change. We'll be focusing on the things we can control, not those we can't. We can be fully engaged in life and relationships without being attached to them. True love and caring are not based on attachment; instead, they are rooted in the desire to be the best person we can be and to bring as much joy and as many blessings to others as possible. That is how we fully engage: by fully evolving and becoming a miracle for the people we care about.

Attachment is about dependence. It's about not being able to let go of something or someone because we have let that something or someone define a part of who we are. This can be a brutal truth to realize, but that doesn't make it any less valid. Being detached means that if you are in a completely fulfilled relationship with your spouse, and when he or she dies, you don't cease to exist. You grieve, certainly, because that is part of being human, but you don't let the loss of any relationship take away your sense of self. You don't spend your time asking unanswerable questions like, "Why me?" Dwelling on questions that have no reasonable answer is focusing on things we can't control. In *Lifeonomics*, we do what it takes to heal (and we're not minimizing that—it's hard work), we move on, we refuse to keep feeding obsessive thoughts and we continue to grow.

If you're not able to heal, a good question to ask is, "Why am I still dwelling on this?" and consider therapy the safest place to ask the "Why?" question. If you're going to do so, you might need professional help so it's not going off the rails. Relegating the question to a particular time, such as the 50 minutes you spend with your therapist every week, keeps it from becoming a constant obsession and allows you to get helpful feedback. Thinking of something over and over again doesn't produce any new change. What does help us is taking the day-to-day action of realizing we've taken everything we can from this and are now focusing elsewhere.

Although many people hesitate to spend money on a therapist, think of it as an investment in your overall health and productivity. Your therapist can be an important part of your life team. By reframing situations a little bit and helping you look at them differently, a good therapist can help you find better solutions and reduce your overall stress. Studies show that

60—80% of all medical diagnoses have a stress component. If we reduce stress, think of the return on our health. If you don't have a therapist, you may be able to achieve a similar benefit from a committed relationship with someone who has agreed to tell you the truth when you need to hear it. One best practice is to have them ask you first if you're open to hearing what they have to say. Timing is everything.

Keep in mind that any breakdowns in life, including someone else's breakdown, can be costly in terms of productivity and money and put us in a situation where we take bad advice, including the advice spinning around in our head. If we're only functioning at 80% because we're caught up in obsessing about a problem, imagine what would happen if we could function at 100%? Failing to address underlying problems can leave us vulnerable to turning to the many things people use to make themselves feel better, like self-medication, which can lead to addiction, as we discussed in the chapter on boundaries.

In the case of grieving, letting it go doesn't mean we loved the person any less, only that our sense of identity was not tied to that other person and that we choose to live in the present. When Tom Cruise said, "You complete me" in the movie *Jerry Maguire*, he was expressing a profoundly unhealthy sentiment. If we need someone or something to complete us, we are too attached. Detachment is being complete unto yourself, completely able to feel the emotional tides of living, but not willing to lose yourself in anything or anyone else.

This is not to say that detachment is easy. If we've had a traumatic loss of a loved one, for instance, we can't just tell ourselves to "snap out of it" and expect to move on. It takes a conscious, ongoing effort. Someone who is grieving may not be able to get away from the grief for months or years, but with time, they may be able to make a conscious decision to put it out of their mind for the next two hours to enjoy a family member's birthday party and be present for everyone who is there. As more time passes, it may be possible to go for longer stretches without the pain of grief overwhelming what is going on in the present. Sometimes, we need help, however. If we notice that we keep getting pulled back into rumination and have a problem with letting go of a particular thing, that's an indicator light that maybe we need to look into this more deeply and seek counsel.

Sometimes, we may face ongoing situations that we can't easily let go of. For instance, if a family member has a chronic health condition and needs care, or someone we love is struggling with a problem like addiction, it will likely always be present as long as we are connected to that person. In cases like this, Letting It Go is about making a conscious effort to focus on the problem when we are dealing with it, but to Let It Go when we are involved with other things, like spending time with other loved ones, working, exercising or other activities, so we can be fully present. That will give us the breaks we need to refresh our mindset so we can truly be there for the individual who needs help without burnout.

Scientists think that meditation could join Sudoku and crossword puzzles as ways of training your brain to be more active and supple as you get older. According to the book The Physical and Psychological Effects of Meditation by Michael Murphy and Steven Donovan, regular meditators have better powers of concentration and faster reaction times than non-meditators.

"Why me?" can be the worst question we can ask when something goes wrong in our lives. We would like to see you turn your life into a "No-Why Zone." I understand that we ask the question to help us grasp the reason behind the things that happen, especially when bad things happen to good people. But we're not always evolved enough to comprehend the answer! We don't even fully understand how our brains or nature work, so why would we be able to untangle the web of cause and effect that ends up defining the highs and lows of our lives? What makes us think we can look back and identify the critical junctures where one decision or another led to the dissolution of a marriage or the loss of a job?

Of course, that doesn't stop us from trying. Asking "Why?" when something happened won't bring you relevant insight and is also the worst form of attachment. It's not that you shouldn't be asking, "what" decisions or choices led someone to have a heart attack or get into a car accident. Part of learning from life's events is identifying actions or patterns of decision-making that have caused trouble in the past and finding ways to avoid repeating them. That's positive. What is not productive is asking "Why?" to figure out what an event *means*, what it says about you, or why God or the Universe chose to inflict this pain on you.

We want to believe that the worst tragedies we encounter, such as the death of a child, must have a reason behind them because it's terrifying to think they might be random. There may well be purpose and meaning behind such things—an order or a plan—but I don't believe that we can fully understand what it is. In that case, obsessing over the meaning of life's events becomes a kind of self-torment.

True suffering comes from emotional attachment to the things that happen to us, replaying them again and again in our minds and asking the worst kinds of unanswerable questions:

> *"Why do things like this always happen to me?"*
> *"Why is God punishing me?"*
> *"What did I do in my life to deserve this?"*

There's no answer to such questions. They lead to nothing. They heal nothing. Rather, they cripple. They foster circular thinking, endless grief and, at their worst, denial of reality, which impedes our ability to grow and adapt to life. It's normal and understandable to feel grief, shock, or fear during a difficult life event. That's our body's physical response to the thoughts produced by wrenching, sudden change or loss. However, in the long run, we've got to heal and escape the gravitational pull of "Why?" The alternative is to get sucked in by suffering that has no benefit whatsoever. The only way to live a spiritually healthy life is to consciously choose in each moment whether to fully live in the present or ruminate on the past. For some people, setting a time limit on ruminations is a step in the right direction. They allow themselves to obsess for 30 minutes but no longer. Eventually, this practice can free them from doing so altogether.

Burning Your Regrets

Lifeonomics is about breaking free of worry and regret. When we let go of our attachments, we will let go of regret. That's the incredible power of Letting It Be, Learning From It and Letting Go. It frees us to say, "I'm not going to focus on that anymore," because we know we have moved on. We are no longer the person we were when something regrettable occurred. We know that we will not repeat anything that may have contributed to adversity because of how much we have grown. So, there's no need to go on punishing ourselves for it. We can take pride in our growth and new wisdom.

To facilitate this, I suggest a little ceremony. Life these days is sadly short on ceremony, which is one reason there's a growing movement among men and women who engage in wilderness treks that involve the ancient ceremonies of indigenous peoples and rituals, such as the vision quest, where people spend time in the wilderness fasting in solitude. Ceremonies mark moments of passage in our lives, which I think is healthy and necessary. So, to mark the letting go of your regrets, I suggest burning your regrets in effigy. Seriously. Write a list of all the things that you regret. Then, hold the paper aloft and say with great seriousness, "I forgive myself for all of these things, I am free of regret for them," then light the paper on fire and Let It Go. Do this somewhere safe. We don't want our regret-burning ceremony to create a whole new regret that needs burning!

This may seem silly, but such gestures matter. We spend so much time gathering our regrets, as squirrels gather nuts, that we don't think about the process, much less what it is doing to our peace of mind. When we become *mindful* of the act of harboring regret, it is easier to let the regrets go. What better way to become mindful than to hold a little impromptu "regret barbecue?" When we become more conscious of any unconscious process, we become, by definition, more aware of it. When we are aware that we must avoid attachment to avoid collecting new regrets, and when we let go of the old ones we've stored away, we can truly live without regret.

This act is what the Bible calls *metanoia,* but, unfortunately, is often simply translated as *repentance,* which some believe does a disservice to the original Greek. Now, try to set aside any preconceptions you might have about what that word means. It does not mean being really, really sorry for something. Many believe the original Greek meaning of the word was simply "turn away from or to change one's mind." When a small child outgrows a toy, he or she simply puts it down and turns away from it, moving on to something else. There's no shame or guilt in it; they just Let It Go. But when we become adults, we attach all sorts of baggage to the things we do and the choices we make. We get caught up in what we think we're supposed to do, the expectations of others, our political or religious values and so on. It gets to the point that doing what's best for us—which is one of the only things we can control —becomes something that we feel we have to *apologize* for. We think that's ridiculous.

In burning our regrets, we physically and emotionally repent for the mistakes of our past—we turn away from them and let them go because we simply don't need them anymore. That's a powerful act of self-love and a declaration of our own importance.

Exercise: Plan Your Regret Burning Ceremony

We suffer from a profound lack of ritual in our society, but you don't have to. Develop a personal ritual to recognize regrets and then burn and release them. It can incorporate your faith, such as Christianity, or anything else you wish. Download the sheet by going to www.Lifeonomics.com.

Plan Your Regret Burning Ceremony	
Where will your ceremony take place?	
Who will be there?	
What will you do as your ritual?	
What past regrets will you let go of?	
How will this ceremony change you?	

The river's gone dry. A dam's been done, of callouses, scabs and scars
Shown with pride, the perfect place to hide.
And so is built the solitary cell.
By the hands of the prisoner.
By design of Hell
So when the coming together misses the mark,
The soul cries for freedom, but it's afraid of the dark.

—Rob Holdford, from "The Coming Together"

Open the prison door

So many people live with a clenched fist in their chest, weighed down by the burdens of their past and the guilt or grief they think they are obligated to carry around. If this is you, the simple question I have to ask is, "How's that working out for you?" Is carrying around grudges, obligations, pain, or resentment from 20 or 30 years ago making your life happier? Is it empowering you to be a better person? Or does it have you in a self-built prison, limiting what you believe you're capable of?

Attachment to past pain or guilt is the only kind of prison where every inmate is given the key to the front door. We all have the power to let ourselves out, to let it go and realize we can't go back and rewrite the beginning of our story. Fortunately, we can rewrite the ending. When we find it in ourselves to Let It Go, it's like that clenched fist opens into a palm, the universal sign of peace. The tension, rage, pain and fear drift away on the breeze. It's often the things we most need to release that we're clenching most tightly. We realize that it's OK to lighten up and not take things (or ourselves) so seriously. There's only so much attention, energy and time we can devote to things we cannot change. The thing that is most out of our control is the past. Not only do bad things happen, but good things happen, as well. Miracles come to pass. That's the release of an enormous burden.

Now that we understand this step in the ***Lifeonomics*** process, it's time to move on to the last one. Let's talk about mindfulness and living in the now, the part of this book that will bring us closest to reaping the benefits of a 29-hour day.

Summary

- Let It Go means stop paying for past sins.
- Stop letting events define who you are.

- Engaging in life means being the best person you can be for the people who love you.
- Stop asking, "Why?" and focus on "What?"
- We cannot save anyone, and no one can save us; we can only save ourselves.

To-Do List

- Smile as much as possible.
- Turn away from regrets that have been haunting you.
- Help a friend create a ritual to burn his or her regrets.
- Stop looking to others to define or complete us.

CHAPTER EIGHT:

Live Now

"It is not death that men should fear, but he should fear
never beginning to live."
— *Marcus Aurelius*

A few years ago, I was at a bar that was situated on a lake. Late in the evening, two guys got very drunk and decided to go for a little boat ride. Bad idea! It became worse when they headed around the point, misjudged the angle, hit the rocks and crashed into the water. I ran to the end of the point and heard one of the guys screaming for help, saying that they were drowning. I didn't think about anything. I just went into the water, swam 20 yards into the darkness, and, as I reached them, found one guy barely holding up his unconscious friend to keep him from drowning. At the moment I reached them, the conscious guy gave out, and gave up, letting his friend sink. I reached down a foot or two beneath the surface and caught him by his shirt, pulling him back up. A boat pulled up right at that moment and dropped a flotation device down to me. I put the device under my arms, held tight to both of their shirts, all three of us floating face up, and started kicking. These were both 200-pound men, but I guess

God and adrenaline were with me that night as I pulled them both out and saved their lives.

I'm not looking for hero accolades, but I am trying to make a point. While this was going on, I had no fear at all. I was completely lost in the moment. I didn't think about what could happen if I went out to save those guys. I just did it.

If I hadn't been in the moment, I might have frozen by the fear of what might happen if I jumped into the lake, and the guys might have drowned. My wife was freaking out, yelling, "Don't you go in there!" because she wasn't in the moment but was instead thinking about what could happen in the future. Fortunately, I was 100% present in that brief time between jumping in the lake and getting back to shore, towing those two drunk but very lucky fellows.

You may be familiar with the saying that the word "FEAR" is an acronym for "False Evidence Appearing Real." I agree with that. Fear is often just an expression of worry over what might happen in the future, whether it's justified or not. But when we're completely centered in the present moment, fear becomes impossible.

That's not to say you might not have a fear-based reaction to something after the fact. You can read about disasters or police shootouts where the people involved were cool as cucumbers while the violence or destruction was going on because they were focused on survival at the moment. But hour after things were all over, they had a breakdown or went into shock because of the body's delayed reaction to what *might* have happened. Our natural tendency to react fearfully is to look at what just went down and say, "Hey, we could have been killed by that crazy gang member with the Uzi," and bring on a kind of delayed fight, flight, or freeze reaction. If there was ever a time to Let It Go, it's when the firefight is over. You're okay, so what are you worrying about?

From UrbanDharma.com, a description of what meditation is NOT: "We are not going to teach you to contemplate your navel or to chant secret syllables. You are not conquering demons or harnessing invisible energies. There are no colored belts given for your performance, and you don't have to shave your head or wear a turban. You don't even have to give away all your belongings and move to a monastery. In fact, unless your life is immoral and chaotic, you can probably get started right away and make some sort of progress."

Mindfulness

The fourth step in the process of freeing yourself from worry and regret is Live Now. It is also referred to as *mindfulness*. This is a concept that's sometimes associated with Buddhism, but there's nothing exclusively Buddhist about it. Mindfulness just means that we are mindful of where we are in the moment, right now. We stop the endless flow of reflection on the past, worry about the future, criticism, planning and rehashing, and just stay in the present, appreciating what we're doing and feeling it at the very second we're doing and feeling it. That's a hard thing to do. We're programmed by modern life to despise silence and to see sitting around and just letting our minds drift as laziness or even the sin of sloth. But when we consciously quiet the stream of thoughts that run through our mind and just *stay* in the now, worry and regret drop away.

Life happens in the moment. The past is gone and can't be changed, and the future is unknowable and can't be responded to until it happens. We can't change the past or control the future, and what have we learned about things that we can't control? Right, we let them go. Everything that we experience, good and bad, is manifested in an endless series of present moments that rush by us like we're a stone in a stream. When we stop trying to swim so hard, we can feel the silky tug and flow of the water. We can sense the moment and appreciate the wonder of being present in our own lives. The moment is immortal. We find God in the moment, freed from our thoughts, simply being and beholding without opinion or contemplation. It's the closest thing there is to magic.

> *If you want to test your memory, try to recall what*
> *you were worrying about one year ago today.*
>
> —*E. Joseph Cossman, entrepreneur*

Exercise: Be Present For A Day

Being present in the here and now is one of the hardest habits for busy multi-taskers to develop. Once we do learn how, it's one of the best ways to conquer stress and worry and really appreciate the wonders of your life. In this exercise, you take a day to be present as much as possible and write down what you notice. If you'd like more space or to share the exercise with someone, download it from www.Lifeonomics.com.

Be Present For a Day	
My day:	What I saw:
	What I heard:
	What I noticed for the first time:
	What made me laugh or cry:
	How the day changed me:

The author Ambrose Bierce said something profound about living in the moment, though I don't think that's what he was talking about. A determinedly cantankerous man who wrote the sardonic *Devil's Dictionary*, Bierce said that all things in life are enjoyed only in anticipation of the memory. In other words, we can only savor life when we're looking forward to something like a trip or a sporting event, or when we're looking back on it, maybe posting photos on social media, saying, "Wasn't that great?"

Well, Mr. Bierce was an example of someone who did not know how to live in the moment. The truest, deepest joys in life come when you are present: holding your newborn child, listening to a Mozart symphony, watching the sunset over the desert, stopping and hearing a birdsong where you hadn't noticed it before, sliding on a luxurious piece of clothing and feeling the fabric caress your skin, periods of intense gratitude. You might look back on those experiences and smile at the memory, but that's a copy of what happened. Rather than rush past an experience and try to hold onto it in memory, we need to choose to live it fully, savor it like a fresh peach, and then Let It Go and move on to the next moment.

Enjoying the details of life, both big and small, as they are happening brings our minds into the present moment as nothing else can. Try it now: find some mundane object in your house or office that you've seen a million times, but now look at it so that you can really appreciate its shape, color, or texture. Realize that there is nothing else precisely like it in the universe and that the moment you spend appreciating it will never come again. While you're doing this, defer your worries about your bills or feeling bad about that email you sent to your friend earlier in the day.

Mindfulness brings you completely into the now, and that's a worry-free, regret-free zone.

Try something else: Make a list of the most fulfilling things in your life, experiences that bring you completely into the moment. You'll probably be surprised how many there are.

Talk about believing we have control over external events: Experiments have shown that when rolling the dice in craps, people tend to throw harder for high numbers and softer for low numbers. Under some circumstances, the subjects of experiments have been made to believe that they could affect the outcome of a random dice toss. Subjects who guessed a series of coin tosses more successfully began to think that they were actually better guessers than others and believed that their performance would be less accurate if they were distracted. Either they're psychic or just really, really need to believe they can control things.

We're Just Playing the Odds

After we Let It Be, Learn From It and Let It Go, Live Now is the logical conclusion to the L Step process. Why? Because doing so prevents us from falling back into patterns of obsessing over the past or future. When we live primarily in the past or future, we're cheating ourselves of the wonders of the now. Regret and worry are thieves that steal our ability to truly experience babies' first steps, meteor showers and cleanly turned double plays—and the many other experiences that bring so much delight to living. Worry and regret are manifestations of fear, and fear is, at its heart, the absence of love. That absence can only exist when we are projecting into a future that doesn't exist yet or are looking back at a past we cannot change. It has no place in the now.

So why do our minds get stuck in yesterday or tomorrow? I believe we harbor the delusion that punishing ourselves with regret over the past will absolve us of unwise choices and that we can control the future. Part of living now is letting go of the idea that we can control our future, because we can't. We can plan to create a track to run on so we know if we're off track, but we have to accept that life will bring unexpected events that require us to assess and adjust our plans. We can plan, prepare and anticipate, but that's not the same thing.

My business is financial planning and wealth management, so let me pull an example from that world. As a couple approaches retirement, they often get more anxious about the possibility of a stock market downturn. So, one of the things I do is help them prepare and protect themselves as best I can against that possibility. Together, we work to make sure they have as little debt as possible, that they are saving as much for retirement as they can, that their insurance is up to date and that their portfolio is well-diversified. Great. But all I'm doing is giving them better odds of making it through a disaster—I'm not preventing one. If the stock market collapses, they're still going to take a hit. If the husband has a stroke at 55, they're going to lose his income for a while, maybe permanently, if he's too disabled to work. All I can do is improve their odds of getting through tough times, and if the tough times don't come, then they will be more prosperous. That's all that your physician, lawyer, or insurance agent can do, as well. We don't have control over what will happen.

I think that reality scares people, especially successful ones who are used to believing they can control events. Some have trouble breaking out of old habits. People who are used to worrying about tomorrow sometimes feel that if they give that up and center their minds in the now, they are somehow "neglecting" their futures, as though bad things are more likely to happen if you're not worrying about them. I think it's time for our first *Lifeonomics* Law, and it relates to the odds of misfortune:

Lifeonomics™ *Law #1:*

What will happen tomorrow is almost never as bad as we fear it will be.

Yes, bad stuff happens. Yes, kids get cancer, planes crash, people lose their jobs and get held up at gunpoint. But the odds of those things happening to you are pretty small. They seem like they happen more frequently than they do because we live in a 24/7 news world now, and hear about them more often. In our grandparents' generation, people didn't even know a relative had died for weeks or months because a letter had to travel by hand from one location to another to carry the news. Now, we *actually see* horrible things as they happen on the Internet, social media, or cable TV. That doesn't mean they will happen to us. Odds are, they're not going to. Your cholesterol might be a little high, but you're probably not going to drop dead tomorrow from a heart attack. You might hate flying, but your plane is going to land just fine if a little late. Bad things probably aren't going to happen. If they do, you can handle them. That's it. That's the magic equation that frees you from the responsibility for worrying so that you can be here now, living in the "holy moment."

Cultivating Mindfulness

Living Now is the final stage of the process of saying goodbye to worry and regret, so it's where all the rewards reside. In training ourselves to accept the events of our lives as they are, without judgment, and learn from them to become better and wiser, we gain the ability to live in the moment and enjoy all that it has to offer. What benefits can you enjoy from living mindfully? The only question is where to start, but here's a sampling:

- **Reduced anxiety**—Anxiety is a cyclical, obsessive worry often over things that are extremely unlikely to occur. When it becomes pervasive enough, it's labeled as a disorder. But anxiety can only occur when we let our minds drift into the uncertain future and become fearful of remote possibilities. Existing primarily in the now and focusing our mind on what is happening today—knowing that tomorrow will take care of itself—reduces the possibility of anxiety because our mind is occupied with the present and can't step onto that worrisome treadmill to start obsessing.
- **Greater gratitude**—It's amazing what we become grateful for when we step out of the perceptual stream of time and just exist

in the now. When we look around at where we are and what we're doing and appreciate how we feel, we realize that everything is something to be grateful for: the breath in your lungs, the people around us, the sun or clouds in the sky, the texture of the clothes we're wearing, the sounds of traffic. It's all rare and marvelous and precious, and when we stop living backward or forward and stay in the moment, we can feel gratitude for being alive and aware in this place, in this time.

- **Less stress**—Stress comes when our illusion of being in control of things is thwarted by the reality that we're not in control. So, when traffic bogs down and we're late for a meeting, we become stressed because we think somehow that traffic *owes* it to us to flow smoothly. Or, when the stock market tumbles and our retirement account temporarily loses value, we become stressed because we thought that we could prevent losses with sound planning. And so on. Aside from giving up the delusion that we are in control of anything but our own words, thoughts and actions, we can reduce stress by bringing our attention to what is happening in the now and appreciating that there is value and wonder in even a situation that appears negative on the surface—if we choose to see it.

- **Keener awareness**—Do you fail to notice what others find obvious? Do you not remember names or miss details that you needed to be aware of? You're probably not suffering from dementia, but just have your mind so embedded in the past and future that you have little left for now, other than to experience it on autopilot. Mindfulness is like taking your mind off autopilot and waking up to what is around you at any given moment. When we do that, we'll be more aware of details, names, signs and clues to what's going on with people and events. We'll find our perceptions sharper and more productive.

- **Wiser decisions**—Fear and worry distort reality, and distortion leads to unsound decision-making. For instance, if we harbor an irrational fear that an earthquake will destroy our homes, even though we live in an area where earthquakes are almost unknown, we might waste hundreds or thousands of dollars on useless earthquake insurance. But when we live in the moment, fear and worry drift away like smoke on the breeze. We're focused on what we need to do now, so irrational worries don't distort our thinking.

- **Deeper spirituality**—Whatever spiritual tradition you come from, you'll find your spiritual sense deepened by attention to the present moment. In the now is where we find awe, wonder, peace, beauty and a sense of oneness with all things and people. It's where the cognitive mind ceases its chatter, and we can simply open ourselves to what is. Mindfulness opens us to the nature of creation and the astonishing reality of the things and people around us and our relationship with them. It's a wonderful addition to whatever meditative or spiritual practice you have in your life today.

So, how can you cultivate mindfulness and Live Now, consciously and attentively? First, understand that mindful living is a discipline like martial arts. It won't happen overnight. Your mind is habituated toward reliving the past and anticipating the future. It will take time to break that habit. Also, you can't live in the moment all the time, even if you want to. There are times when it's good to remember a past lesson or fact or to plan for the future. That said, you can make living in the now your mind's new "default." The way to do that is to create methods and reminders in your life that help bring you into the present. Remember, if you can't act in your best interest, then it's up to you to create foolproof systems that get you to take the necessary action, like hiring a personal trainer. It's the result that matters, not the method.

The greatest mistake you can make in life
is to be continually fearing you will make one.

—Elbert Hubbard, <u>*The Note Book of Elbert Hubbard*</u>

Exercise: Five Things That Distract My Mind

The hardest part about cultivating mindfulness is that we let ourselves be pulled from the moment by any number of distractions: the news, money worries, old arguments. What distracts you, and what can you do about it? For more, download this worksheet from www.Lifeonomics.com.

Five Things That Distract My Mind	
Distraction:	What I can do to prevent it:
Distraction:	What I can do to prevent it:
Distraction:	What I can do to prevent it:
Distraction:	What I can do to prevent it:
Distraction:	What I can do to prevent it:

One of the best ways to develop the habit of mindfulness—the one I use most often—is to permit people to remind you to be in the moment. Literally, tell the people who are closest to you or whom you see most often that you're trying to be more "in the now." If they notice you drifting into regret or worry, give them carte blanche to ask, "Where are you right now?" That's a great wake-up call and always brings my attention roaring back to the present. I love to answer, "Right here, right now, my brother/sister!" Also, try focusing on helping someone else. This works wonders. The next time you know somebody who is caught up in fear and worry, distract them by allowing them to help someone else. They will forget about their fears. Try it, and you'll see the effects.

Another trick is to post physical reminders around your home or working space. I mean written notes, a screen saver that you can customize, the wallpaper on your cell phone—write notes that say things like, "Be in the moment." You can also write a morning affirmation that you say each day when you get up, something like, "Today, I will attend to, live in and appreciate the moment as it comes as often as possible." I also suggest keeping a daily journal starting now so that instead of dwelling on the past, you can keep an accurate record of it.

As time goes by, you'll get better at this. You'll slowly reprogram your brain to be less focused on the stream of time before or behind you and more focused on the present. What a great way to live!

What's Your Purpose?

When I began working with Amy Constable, during her time with Carson Wealth Management as a Foundational Partner, her four-year romantic relationship had just ended. Although she found her work challenging, she realized she lacked a strong sense of internal purpose—the answers to questions like "Why am I here?" "Why am I doing the things I do?"

She understood how that had happened during her relationship. Her boyfriend had been heavily involved in the self-development movement, particularly with Tony Robbins, and had constantly pushed her to follow his lead. This had led to an overwhelming feeling of burden, as if she were never living up to his standards.

"During that time, I so wanted the relationship to be what it wasn't that I lost myself in it," she recalls. "When it ended, I almost didn't know who I was anymore."

Working with me and what we now call the **Lifeonomics** *Process to Purpose*, Amy developed a purpose statement that she decided she would use as a compass to drive all the decisions in her life. "Coming out of that relationship, I learned that your purpose should be centered around something bigger than another person," she says.

To come up with the statement, I asked her to envision where she saw herself 25 years in the future. Who were the 'A' relationships—people who knew her well, understood her purpose and supported her in that?

Her purpose included several key statements:

- Glorify God
- Love passionately and unconditionally
- Learn, give and serve
- Appreciate and embrace the journey
- Inspire.

Today, Amy uses the purpose statement to guide her life. "I feel like I have grounding," she says. "I know who I am, what my boundaries are and the things I want out of life. It's been helpful to make better decisions."

That has played out in many parts of her life, including her relationships. "When I see my friends who are coming out of relationships and jumping into the next thing, it makes me sad," she says. "I would love for them to take time for themselves and learn about who they are and what they want. That's something I have the opportunity to do now."

Early in the book, we talked about the fact that the real goal of living should be to do what is most important to you with the people who matter most to you. I have another name for that: finding your purpose. We all need purpose in life, and I don't think it's given to us automatically by any divine power. We have to explore and figure out what it is, and that journey makes us stronger and wiser. once you've found your purpose, it will bring you into the present more powerfully than anything else. This is how **Lifeonomics** defines purpose: *Purpose is that which gives meaning to your now.*

Let me explain. When we live in the present, it's amazing and life-changing. However, that doesn't necessarily mean we see that we have a reason for watching that sunset or playing that guitar. Purpose changes all that. Purpose is the thing that we feel we are meant to do, the thing that's most important to us (which may have nothing to do with money, by the way). When our moments have purpose because we spend them doing what's Truly Important to us with the people who are Truly Important to us, then we are doing something to make a positive difference in the world. The word "meaning" gets tossed around a great deal, but it is simply knowing that we are having a beneficial effect on the world in some way, being a blessing to someone or something. Meaningful time changes the world for the good. Purpose creates meaning, and meaning brings us into the moment because it feels so great to be

When your now is more meaningful than your past or future, you'll build a vacation house there.

So, it's time to ask yourself, "What's most important to you?" What could be your purpose, the thing that creates meaning for you? For many people, raising a family is one of the most important things. After all, raising good kids who become great adults is a powerful way to change the world. If you're older and your kids are grown, maybe your purpose is something else, like giving back to your community or a charity. What is it? Here are some questions that might help you find the answer:

- If you could have all of the money that you need, what would you do? Where would you go? How would you spend your life?
- What would you attempt if you knew you could not fail?
- What do you like the most about your life as it is now? What do you think needs the most improvement?
- What would you have to do to die without regret?
- Where will you have to be personally and financially in five years for you to feel satisfied with your progress?
- What would you like to leave as your legacy?
- What do you consider the greatest injustice in the world? What would you do about it if you could?
- What do you worry about the most? What are you most afraid of?
- What are your biggest regrets? What can you do about them?
- What is the one thing that you have always wanted to do but never have?
- On a scale of 1 to 10, how much joy do you experience in your life?
- What's more important to you, money, things, or experiences?
- What's more important, material comfort or simplicity and tranquility?
- What would you be willing to give up if it meant complete financial freedom from that point on?

In my career, I have never seen anything more powerful than when a person clearly defines and aligns with their life's purpose. Some examples:

- Time with family
- Learning
- Creating
- Traveling
- Proclaiming
- Playing
- Competing
- Helping
- Teaching
- Charity
- Leisure
- Meditation
- Discovering
- Inventing
- Improving spiritually
- Improving physically
- Meeting new people
- Building new relationships
- Enriching existing relationships
- Communicating effectively
- Laughing
- Relationships
- Thinking and creating
- Security
- Politics
- Activism

- Making a difference
- Helping in the community

What's the purpose that could create a lifetime of meaningful moments for you? You're already on the way to finding it. Let's keep going.

Summary

- Live Now means being completely in the present moment.
- There is no fear in the now.
- Worry and regret are manifestations of fear.
- All you can do is improve your odds of avoiding disaster in life.
- What will happen is rarely as dire as your imagination makes it.
- Mindful living is the key to happiness.
- Permit people to remind you to be in the moment.
- You must find your purpose to truly live without worry or regret.

To-Do List

- Make a list of things we can do to improve our odds of dodging trouble.
- Appoint three people as our "mindfulness reminders."
- Write down the pursuits that might be our life's purpose.
- Do something that serves our passion.

CHAPTER NINE:

Create Your Life Team

When we turn to one another for counsel,
we reduce the number of our enemies.

—*Kahlil Gibran*

I don't know anything about cars. I can change my oil (barely), but when it comes to today's computerized and micro-engineered vehicles, I'm clueless. Fortunately, that's okay because I have a great mechanic who takes good care of my car, so I can rely on it. It's worth it to pay him his going rate because not only can his preventive maintenance help me avoid breakdowns and expensive problems later on, but he knows how to do the same work I could do, better than I can, in about 20% of the time. My time is valuable, and I prefer to spend it doing what I do best. That's why I seek the good counsel of my mechanic.

I do the same in almost every other area of my life where I need to make good decisions, but lack the expertise to do that without spending hours cramming new information into my mind and teaching myself a whole new discipline. I've found that building what I call a Life Team is an important way to protect my time and energy, allowing me to be more mindful. It's hard to pay attention to what's going on around me if, in addition to running my businesses and living my family life, I've got to find time to watch 10 YouTube videos on engine repair and spend Saturday on the driveway tinkering with my car and hoping for the best. I recommend that all of my clients take the same approach and build their own Life Team. This brain trust will help you answer an important question: *How do we create a structure and method for life that allows us to live free of worry and regret in such a complex world?*

To Let It Be, Learn From It and use all the rest of the steps we've shared with you for building a fulfilling psychological, emotional and spiritual life, begin putting your own foundation in place for your professional, personal, financial, physical and legal life that keeps you prepared for what could happen and doesn't leave you vulnerable. Seeking good counsel—having a Life Team of experts in your life who are strong where you're weak—will help you prepare so that whatever happens, you can respond in the healthiest, most positive way possible.

Be Careful Who You Listen To

The idea of seeking good counsel goes back at least as far as the ancient Chinese philosopher Confucius and refers to a cadre of wise, learned people who would sit with a leader to provide advice and wisdom from their areas of knowledge. From the Knights of the Round Table to the Last Supper, history is filled with images of leaders and their wise counselors. No matter how smart anyone is, no one knows everything. Even a Nobel Prize-winning economist may not know anything about fixing his computer or suing someone. Just as important, we cannot be objective when making decisions about our lives. It's impossible. We're too close to our own lives to have an objective perspective, so we must rely on counselors to give us beneficial advice. That's a Life Team.

This chapter is all about how to build a foundation of relationships with experts who will bring needed knowledge and objectivity to areas of your life that are vital to your immediate and long-term ability to deal with what life throws at you and advocate for you. There are two benefits to creating a Life Team of advocates:

1. **They help you identify small problems before they become big problems.** This comes into play, for instance, when your doctor tells you your cholesterol is getting too high, so you can lose some weight and bring it down. Or when your lawyer warns you that some aspect of your business is leaving you open to a lawsuit, so you can correct it.

2. **They help you lay down a safety net of preparation** so you can best respond to adversity. A perfect example of this is having a great insurance agent who helps you get the right health, life and disability coverage so that no matter what happens, you'll be okay financially.

Much as you might like to rely on friends or family members as advocates, it generally isn't a good idea to place them in this role. People who are close to us may not feel comfortable telling us the truth. Sometimes, our family and friends may be enabling the destructive choices we're making. That's not to mention that our friends and family may need to make a living. Someone who is donating their time may not be able to give our life decisions the time they deserve.

That's why a Life Team should be made up of paid professionals whom we give permission to intervene in our lives—people who will tell us the truth no matter how uncomfortable it makes us in the short term. Professionals in any field know that some short-term discomfort is often the key to opening eyes and making changes that deliver great results in the long term.

In creating a Life Team, be careful who you decide to listen to. Once you choose the right people, listen to them carefully. Referrals from someone you trust are the best way to find a service provider in almost any field, but in the end, trust your instincts. An expert who did a great job for your friend may not be the best fit for you. You are under no obligation to choose an expert after an initial consultation if you feel hesitant about moving forward. Your only obligation is to yourself and your family.

Second, always weigh the value of a referral against the judgment and condition of the person who referred you.

In the search for experts, we also recommend just talking to everyone you meet. I'm lucky enough to have the gift of gab. I can sit down on a plane next to a stranger and by the time we land, they will have told me things their spouse doesn't know. It's an incredible way to form fruitful relationships of all kinds.

I know of a gentleman who makes this part of his sales strategy, and it is very effective. He works in Times Square in New York. His sole method of getting new sales leads is this: He hangs around outside the swanky hotels near Times Square and shares a cab with a man or woman in an expensive suit who is coming out of one of the hotels. Experience has taught him that, much of the time, that person will be a CEO or other high-level executive at a major corporation. This way, he gets 30 minutes of uninterrupted time with a top executive in the back of a cab. He's closed countless deals this way. So, talk with people, even if you don't think they can be directly helpful as a counselor. You never know who they know.

When the right person is found, we recommend taking a step that can be unnerving yet empowering: allowing that professional to hold you accountable in their area of expertise. Allow your financial advisor to call you on the carpet for not saving enough for your retirement, or your IT professional to bug you to install the new virus protection software and firewall before it's too late and someone steals your identity. Part of good counsel is that it holds you to a high standard for your own behavior and decisions, even if you might feel like telling the counselor to mind his own business from time to time.

> *"It only seems as if you are doing something*
> *when you're worrying."*
>
> —*Lucy Maud Montgomery*
> *Author of Anne of Green Gables*

Your Round Table

So, King Arthur, how wilt thou go about assembling thy all-star Life Team of wise advisors for thy Round Table? Well, the first thing is to know which professions we need around our table. Then, we'll talk about how to select them. I've divided my list of key advocates into two groups: "must-haves" and "good ideas." The first are people who are mandatory if we want to live without worry and regret, and be prepared for life's ups and downs. The second are professionals who will benefit about 80% of readers, but may not be for everyone.

Must-Haves

- **A personal physician**. Obviously, you need to care for your health and prevent rather than treat disease. I would also include an eye doctor and a dentist here, and if you are into such things, maybe a chiropractor, acupuncturist, massage therapist, or nutritionist.
- **A lawyer or law firm.** A good lawyer is someone you hope you'll never need, but almost everyone does. Estate planning, family law, contract law and tax law are the most common instances where people need legal advice.
- **A financial or wealth advisor**. I'm biased here, but you simply can't make a long-term plan without a comprehensive understanding of today's complex financial markets.
- **A property and casualty insurance agent.** Having solid health, auto, life, home and disability insurance is critical, and a great agent

will help you navigate the many choices and keep your coverage current. For the self-employed, membership in a trade association may give you access to benefits that are hard to purchase when you are not part of a large group.

- **A good Certified Public Accountant**, especially if you're in business for yourself. They can help you avoid pain in a lot more ways than just doing your taxes.

Good Ideas

- **A therapist and/or spiritual advisor**. Everyone needs someone to talk to from time to time. If you're fundamentally healthy but need a listener on occasion, talk to your pastor, priest, or mullah. If you need more serious help, a therapist or psychologist can work wonders. Look for people with either a Ph.D. or a master's degree, like MFT (marriage and family therapist) or MLSW (licensed social worker).

- **A reliable banker.** Bankers are somewhat forgotten in this day and age of DIY online banking, but there's no substitute for the advice of someone who knows the banking and lending business.

- **A handyman (or woman).** Unless *you're* very handy, you've probably got more projects than you know what to do with and no time to do them. Be sure the person is licensed in your state and bonded.

- **A fitness trainer**. Do you have the discipline to get up at 5 a.m. and work out? Neither do I. I've gotten in shape by using a trainer.

- **An auto mechanic.** Very important, as I mentioned earlier.

- **An IT professional.** Most of us are dependent on computers today, and if the confounding things go down, we're clueless. They're as complex as the human body. That's why a tech geek can be your best friend.

- **A life and business coach**. Most people don't think about this, but it's been a boon to me. Ron Carson, founder and Chairman of Carson Group, and Scott Ford, managing director, partner and wealth advisor at Carson Wealth, have been great mentors and coaches to me as I've built my wealth management practice. A coach is one of the most worthwhile allies you can have in making sure every aspect of your life is on the right path.

How long should it take you to put together your team of wise counselors? I would say six months to a year. You probably have some of them already, and others you may have no idea how to find. Take your time and ask around. Some of the professionals whom you already know and trust may be able to refer you to others. Maybe your family physician knows a great personal trainer. That synergistic quality of good counselor relationships is one of the true blessings of this whole concept of creating a "Life Team" of advocates.

When you begin to work with an advocate in almost any field, you have an immediate, personal relationship with that individual. He or she becomes what I call a *primary advocate*. This is your lawyer, your financial advisor, or your therapist. In almost every case, this individual will have advocates he or she works with, people who will provide information to your advocate to pass along to you, though you may never meet them. These are *secondary advocates,* and they form a huge part of what becomes a sort of perfect storm of information and guidance swirling around you at the center.

For example, in my financial practice, as a member of Carson Group Partners, I have access to a large team of independent researchers—economists, money managers and so on—doing due diligence research on markets, technologies and legislative risk that they give me so I can help my clients make better decisions. My clients may never meet these people, but they have access to them and their knowledge *through me.* One advocate can be an indirect source for many others who can enhance your life.

Exercise: My Life Team List

You may already have a Life Team, at least in part. But few people have all the professionals they need to live a life free of worry and regret. Write down the people on your team today and check off the ones you still need to find. If you'd like a larger version, download it from www.Lifeonomics.com.

My Life Team List			
Team Member	**I have this person Y/N**	**If yes, name & contact info**	**If no, any prospects?**
Family Physician			
Attorney			
Financial Advisor			
Insurance Agents			
CPA			
Therapist			
Banker			

My Life Team List			
Team Member	**I have this person Y/N**	**If yes, name & contact info**	**If no, any prospects?**
Handyman			
Auto Mechanic			
IT Professional			
Life Coach			
Hair Stylist			
Dentist			
Medical Specialists			

Absolute Honor

Of course, the key issue is choosing the right professionals with whom we can have a productive and mutually satisfying relationship for many years. Let's face it, having the wrong lawyer or financial advisor can really screw up your life, so these aren't easy choices. And while you can always dump your doctor and find a new one if you want to, why would you go to all that trouble? Why not make a sound decision in the first place?

In choosing people for your team of wise counselors, experience matters. I wouldn't go to a doctor straight out of medical school or a lawyer who had just passed the bar. I want someone who has been around the block and learned the most valuable asset in any profession: creative thinking informed by years of seeing what works in the real world. So, you want someone who does what you want a lot and has done it for many years. That's a good benchmark.

But the more important quality that I feel we should all be looking for in our counselors—as well as cultivating in ourselves—is what I call "absolute honor." Honor is an outdated concept in our society, but since we're working on a King Arthur metaphor in this chapter, let's talk about it. Absolute honor is nothing more or less than living by your word, being who you say you are and doing what you say you will do. That is, after all, the only thing each of us has at the end of the day when we lay down the degrees, credentials and titles: our word. In our culture, we've gotten out of the habit of honor and sticking to our word. I feel that we should not promise what we can't deliver, and that if we do overpromise, we come up with a plan to fix things ASAP. That may be an old-fashioned code of conduct, but it's the one I adhere to, and I demand the same from my advocates.

Living with honor is vital from a personal development standpoint, as well as in choosing advisors, because it's training your subconscious. The more you act with integrity, the more you teach your subconscious mind that you are someone who can be trusted and that it's vital to your sense of self to be honorable. On the other hand, if you act without integrity and honor, then you'll teach your subconscious that lesson, breeding more dishonorable behavior. That becomes hypocrisy, which should be the Eighth Deadly Sin. The reason we have the law to govern human activities is that people do not always behave with honor. Honor is each person's constitution or set of principles from which we should never deviate.

So, when you are searching for your advocates, or even when you're reviewing the ones you already have to see if you want to keep them in your life, make honor just as important as experience, perhaps even more so. Get to know your possible advocates and find out what is important to them and what their values are. Learn if they are living in integrity with those values. That matters a great deal. about it: You're going to be trusting your advocates with your health, finances, security and future. You won't be around to supervise them. You HAVE to trust that they will do what they say they will do according to the standards they have set for themselves.

There's a simple way to do this: Ask tough questions. Your potential advocate is going to dig deep into your life, so why shouldn't you do the same? Your financial planner will ask numerous questions about your job, spending habits and financial decisions…your doctor will ask about your family history and diet, and your therapist will be the most intrusive of all, delving into your marriage, childhood, even your sexual habits. Be just as demanding. Your advocates have the potential to bring great blessings to your life or do great harm, and each is an important choice. Write down the questions you want answered, and don't be afraid to ask them. If the person won't answer, then look for someone else.

Beyond Honor

Honor is a pretty lofty requirement for a personal service professional, I'll admit. Others are nearly as important, so let's look at the other things to look for—and avoid. Integrity is a must. In researching and interviewing possible members of your team, I suggest that you watch out for conflicts of interest. The worst example of a conflict of interest was a sign I saw once outside of a shop in a small town. It said, "John Smith –Veterinarian and Taxidermist." His motto was, "Your Pet Goes Home Either Way." (Yes, that was a joke, but it makes the point.)

In my profession, the commission-based stockbroker is going extinct, and for good reason. people make money by actively trading clients' assets and buying and selling shares of stock, for instance. Over-trading your account is called "churning," and it's unethical because it puts the broker's needs before yours. To avoid this scenario, a growing number of wealth managers, including myself, are paid based on the amount of money we manage, so there's no need for us to churn your account.

I also suggest finding a professional who provides you with accountability that is benchmarked in some way. This does not work for all professions—medicine and mental health come to mind—but it does for many. For example, you could require your CPA to deliver to you a quarterly financial statement with strategic recommendations for your business or personal finances, something that not only shows you that the accountant has been doing work on your behalf but also requires him or her to give you extra value. I really believe in this because I think we all tend to get complacent. If a professional has a high overhead, he's going to be carrying a lot of clients and probably assuming he can skate with some of them because they will never ask him to justify the money they're paying him. Don't be one of those clients. Demanding accountability and reporting is not being a pain in the neck; it's just good business.

Choose the roles you need to fill in your life. First, look at the relationships you already have with professionals and ask: "Do they fill this role? Do I trust them?" You need to have faith in their intentions and abilities.

You must believe that their intent aligns with yours and that they care about you and your benefit. It doesn't matter how good they are if they don't care about what you're trying to achieve in life. Second, they must have the ability to benefit you with their knowledge, wisdom and experience.

Finally, ask for references. Just as you cannot be objective about your own life, your counselors cannot be objective about themselves. For objective opinions about their integrity and performance, always get three references from each person you're considering. When you get the references, don't email or text the person. Make the phone call or, even better, set up a video chat if you're comfortable on Zoom or one of the other platforms. There's nothing more revealing than inflection and choice of words when a person is asked to speak about someone else spontaneously. You'll learn a great deal that will help you make a smarter decision and choose truly "wise counselors."

"Worry ducks when purpose flies overhead."

—*C. Astrid Weber, poet*

Exercise: The 3 Kinds Of Wealth

In building your team of advisors, it is important to consider the kind of wealth you want to build in your life. It probably is not all monetary.

There are three types of wealth:

- **Intrinsic**—the aspects of your being inherently worthwhile and valuable;
- **Relationship**—the relationships you have with others that enrich your life; and
- **Financial**—your monetary wealth. Where do you stand with each?

This exercise will help you discover the answer. Download it at www. Lifeonomics.com.

The 3 Kinds of Wealth		
Intrinsic Wealth	List everything about yourself that is an asset: your ideas, imagination, passion, honor, unconditional love, etc. Then write a powerful summary sentence about what is Truly Important about you.	
	Assets	What's Truly Important About Me
Relationship Wealth	Compile a list of everyone you know, separating them into two categories: Business and Personal. Then ask the following about each one: 1. Is this relationship Truly Important to me right now? 2. Could this relationship become Truly Important to me?	
	Personal relationships - - - - - - - -	Important to me?	Could it become important to me?

The 3 Kinds of Wealth	
Financial Wealth	Collect information about every area of your finances for future wealth planning. Annual household income:
	Retirement accounts (location, type, assets):
	Other investments (location, type, assets):
	Other savings:
	Life Insurance (carrier, coverage):
	Homeowner insurance (carrier, coverage):
	Disability insurance (carrier, coverage):
	Real estate owned (location, value, amount owed):
	Credit card debt (cards, APR):
	Other debt:

Goodbye, Worry

Seems like a lot of work, doesn't it? Interviewing people, getting referrals, checking references…is it all necessary? Well, that depends on how committed you are to living without worry and regret.

Having a Life Team of good, smart counselors on your side is a big part of saying farewell to worry and regret. These people are your safety net, helping you prepare for possible adversity by making plans or laying down legal or financial foundations, preventing small problems from becoming disasters, or assisting you in responding to a difficult episode, such as a lawsuit. Having the Life Team in place, doing their jobs and helping you live your life more wisely, can help you set aside worry, because they're doing your worrying for you, so to speak.

Think about how confident you feel driving across the country when you know you've just had your car overhauled by a mechanic you trust. And how nerve-racking it is driving on a snowy back road at night when you haven't had that same level of trustworthy service? The same holds true when it comes to almost any element of your life where planning ahead makes a difference, whether it's financial planning or taking care of your health. With a wealth of solid knowledge in your corner, you're more likely to take pre-emptive steps and make the right calls in advance of important life events, so there's no after-the-fact recrimination. For instance, if you get married without a prenuptial agreement and things get ugly, you're going to regret not being objective enough to sign one. But if you have a lawyer who insists that you draft one on the grounds that "things happen," then if the marriage blows up, you might still feel bad about the relationship ending, but you won't have reason to regret your financial or legal decisions. You can look forward, not back.

A team of good counselors is an essential part of the life of any mature individual. It would be wonderful if life were simple enough that we didn't need an army of financial, legal and medical experts to guide and advise us, but that's not the world we live in. Think of it this way: Your team gives you the best chance of making the most of this complicated world and creating the life of your dreams. Now, let's take one final ride together and talk about leveraging that wisdom and experience and putting together a sound, solid Life Plan.

Summary

- You need a Life Team to bring expertise and objectivity to your planning.
- Advocates help you prevent problems.
- Advocates also give you a life safety net.
- Experience matters.
- You should also seek people who act with honor.
- Weed out conflicts of interest.
- Always get references.
- Once you assemble your team, listen to them.

To-Do List

- Begin asking for referrals for Life Plan team members.
- Set up exploratory calls with potential Life Plan team members.
- Engage potential Life Team members on a short-term project to assess how well you work together.
- Examine the members of your current Life Team and decide which ones to terminate.
- List the areas of your Life Plan that still need completion.

CHAPTER TEN:

Your Life and Legacy Plan

"I believe that the very purpose of life is to be happy. From the very core of our being, we desire contentment. In my own limited experience, I have found that the more we care for the happiness of others, the greater is our own sense of wellbeing. Cultivating a close, warmhearted feeling for others automatically puts the mind at ease. It helps remove whatever fears or insecurities we may have and gives us the strength to cope with any obstacles we encounter. It is the principal source of success in life. Since we are not solely material creatures, it is a mistake to place all our hopes for happiness on external development alone. The key is to develop inner peace."

—The Dalai Lama

Finally, we come to the Life and Legacy Plan portion of our show. This is it, boys and girls, where all the material comes together in one focused, strategic plan for today and tomorrow. If we want to live free of worry and regret, we must have a Life and Legacy Plan in place, along with a team to manage it, so we don't have to. That means having a financial or wealth advisor because creating your future and leaving a gift to others once you're gone typically involves money.

You may bridle at the idea of being boiled down to a financial legacy, so let's remind ourselves what money is. Money is not shallow or deep or meaningful or meaningless: money is a neutral tool that can be used to accomplish what you want to accomplish. People can be shallow or deep, and that can help define what they do with their money. But money is also something else: It is the power to effect change in the world. If you want to help people in Africa, you can make a difference by starting an organization that brings aid, microloans, or farming equipment to impoverished villages. But you have to start with money. Money moves people and goods. Money represents power and freedom, and when you leave a legacy for your heirs, those are the gifts you're giving them: power and freedom.

My team and I have even had clients create family foundations so that their values would be carried on after their lives are over. They designated the causes the foundation supports, and every year, the kids and grandkids get together and vote on the organizations that get the foundation grants. By doing this, they carry on Grandma and Grandpa's legacy and values. It's a wonderful thing. So, before we get started, do not get the wrong idea about being defined by the money you leave behind. Money can represent whatever you want it to represent.

A private family foundation can provide many real financial benefits beyond a legacy. It can give you tax savings, reduce estate tax liability, and even help you avoid capital gains taxes on appreciated assets that you contribute to a charity. It brings all of this while preserving your family name and letting your heirs be part of your vision.

Unique Life, Unique Plan

A Life Plan covers you from cradle to grave, while a Legacy Plan covers you after the grave. Every person needs a plan, but no two plans are alike.

There's no template for creating a blueprint for your future finances and lifestyle, so don't let anyone tell you otherwise. Your perspective on life and goals is not going to be the same as anyone else's, so your Life and Legacy Plan needs to be unique to you. This means forming a relationship with someone interested in more than just maximizing the value of your investment portfolio; it means creating a relationship with a team of professionals in investing, taxation, law, estate planning and insurance. Forty percent of Baby Boomers were retired as of September 2020, according to "Pew Research Center[4]. And the rate of retirement has been picking up. Boomers who don't have a Life and Legacy Plan need one *now*.

Here's what you and your team need to know before building your Life and Legacy Plan:

- Your net worth (assets minus liabilities)
- Your cash flow
- Your time horizons—when do you want to make your big transition?
- Your risk tolerance

You'll notice above that I didn't use the word "retirement," instead choosing "make your big transition." That's because I don't believe in retirement, not in the old sense, anyway. As many people have discovered, the idea of quitting work at 65 and spending the next 30 years watching TV is not only insufferably boring, but also a death sentence. The only way to stay alive, vital, healthy, financially well-off and independent is to continue doing something meaningful. I like to use the phrase, "Making the transition from having to work for a living to financial independence." Translation: You can

---

[4] "*The pace of Boomer retirements has accelerated in the past year.*," Pew Research Center. https://www.pewresearch.org/short-reads/2020/11/09/the-pace-of-boomer-retirements-has-accelerated-in-the-past-year/

do what you want to do. If that means spending 10 years practicing your bunker shots, great. It might mean traveling around the world, starting a business or doing charity work. The point is that you have the freedom.

What my team and I look to pinpoint in our work with people who want to create a Life and Legacy Plan is the actual day of that transition. Others might call it their retirement day, the day when they clean out their desk, grab their gold watch and leave the office for the last time, but we're not using the "R" word. Instead, this is what we're trying to define:

The day you know beyond a reasonable doubt that you will be able to spend the time you have left on this earth doing only what is Truly Important to you with the people who are Truly Important to you.

The goal of a Life and Legacy Plan is to get you to that magical point as quickly as possible, then to catapult you past it like a rocket, ready to embark on the next phase of your life and make it whatever

you want it to be. Your goal can be to go from having few choices to having ALL the choices.

It's All About Cash Flow

Investments aren't the key in this grand picture of your future. Life and Legacy Plans revolve around income. We need the income to live the life we have in mind. Everything is about cash flow. To what is Truly Important to you, you need to manage your assets and live a lifestyle that gives you enough cash flow. But first, wipe from your mind any post-work (see, I avoided the "R" word again) income requirements you've heard about. Ignore the chorus of books and experts telling you that you have to have 80% of your income or a million dollars saved to retire. Say goodbye to the antiquated idea of stopping work completely and never earning another dime once you turn 65 or 68. Life after a traditional career looks a lot different today, and the financial requirements have changed dramatically.

Exercise: Describe Your Perfect Retirement Lifestyle

Remember, your post-work life is about a lifestyle first, then working backward to figure out what that lifestyle will cost. This is the time to describe your ideal lifestyle. Download the worksheet at www.Lifeonomics.com.

My Perfect Retirement Lifestyle
What is Truly Important to me?
Who is Truly Important to me?
What am I most passionate about?
What could I spend 30 years doing with unending enthusiasm?

Let me explain some realities:

According to The Pew Research Center, millions of people over 65 are going to continue working in some way, on their own terms, either because

they need the income, they want the extra money, or they just enjoy it and want to keep their minds sharp.[5]
https://www.moneytalksnews.com/millions-of-americans-are-working-past-and-reshaping-the-meaning-of-retirement/)

- Your life and goals are like no one else's, so generic guidelines on what you must save to stop working are worthless.
- Most importantly, all you need to make the transition from working out of need to working out of choice is enough cash flow to allow you to live the life that is important to you. Period.

I have a couple in my financial practice whose grandchildren are what is Truly Important to them. Well, what's important to those kids are sports. Since they have no debt, the grandchildren all live close by and kids' sporting event tickets are pretty inexpensive, this couple only spends about $2,500 a month all in. They attend virtually all their youth soccer games and other sporting events and love every minute of it. That's all they need to lead a life that gives them joy and meaning. Some people might think they're living in poverty in their post-work lives, living on only $30,000 a year, but I think they're rich because they love their lives.

On the flip side, I have clients who came to me to try to figure out how they could cut their monthly expenses from $50,000 to $25,000 so they could survive until their inheritance came in. They had a lifestyle that was important to them, and that's what it cost. We don't judge by what someone spends. Wealth is different for everyone.

Because of this, the **_Lifeonomics_** process for creating a Life and Legacy Plan begins with three fundamental steps:

____

[5] Blythe, K. (2025, June 9). *Millions of Americans are working past 65 and reshaping the meaning of retirement.* Money Talks News. Retrieved from https://www.moneytalksnews.com/millions-of-americans-are-working-past-and-reshaping-the-meaning-of-retirement/

1. **Uncover what is Truly Important to you.** This can take some doing. What could you see yourself spending 20 years doing and never getting tired of doing it? Travel? Starting a small business? Gardening? If you could envision your perfect life after pursuing financial freedom, the life that would give you the most emotional and mental satisfaction and the greatest meaning and purpose, what would it be? When you can answer that question, you're ready for this process.

2. **What is that lifestyle going to cost?** We look at your net income, tax rate, insurance needs, likely inflation and so on. Some lifestyles are going to cost a lot more than others. If you're like my clients whose passion is attending their grandkids' soccer matches, your financial needs may be low. But if you want to spend six months out of every year traveling the world, you and your team need to figure out how to pay for that.

3. **Look at your income sources and figure out, based on that income, what you need** to do and how long you need to work out of need before you can afford the lifestyle that's Truly Important to you. There are three basic income sources:

   a) **Earned income**, which comes from going to a job, is the main source of income for most people

   b) **Direct income**, which comes from sources like Social Security and pensions.

   c) **Capital income**, which means the distributions from your financial investments.

Look at what's Truly Important to you, what it will cost and what income and assets you have. From this information, your team can tell you what you need to live the life of your dreams and how long you'll need to work to build it.

You Don't Know Where You Are Until You Ask

A few years back, I had a gentleman come to my office. He was about 55 and worked at a high-stress job. He was convinced that he had to work at least seven more years before he'd be able to quit and do what he wanted. He was really downcast about it. He told me he had assumed (meaning a bunch of books and TV talking heads had persuaded him) that he needed to save enough money to provide for 80% of his income before he could retire. So, we talked about the lifestyle he and his wife wanted. It was mostly centered around some reasonably priced travel, nothing extravagant. My team ran the numbers based on their assets and income, and in the end, I told him, "John… you have the assets and income to live that lifestyle right now?" He just stared at me for a while, like he didn't believe what I was saying. Then he actually started crying. What I told him had completely changed his expectations for his life. It was one of the most fulfilling moments of my career.

My team and I have retired (I'm going to use the "R" word now because it's simpler, but I still don't like it) hundreds of families over the last 30+ years, and some of them have been able to quit work up to nine years sooner than they expected because we didn't make it about the numbers. In *Lifeonomics*, you don't start with the numbers. You start with what's Truly Important and you back into the numbers. That means your ideal post-work life might have nothing to do with your working income.

Hypothetically speaking, let's say your family's income is $150,000, and that pays for a mortgage, student loans, saving 10% of your income every year in your 401(k), Social Security taxes and so on.

First of all, by the time you hit 60 or so, we may be well on our way to paying off our mortgage or student loans. And remember, after you quit working, you won't be paying Social Security taxes or putting money into your 401(k) anymore. So you'll already be getting a raise just by retiring.

But the key is, the lifestyle you enjoy might cost a lot less than what you live on today. So, don't assume anything, and don't base your presumed ability to leave work behind on what you read in financial books. Ask your wealth advisor and base everything on what is Truly Important to you. If you're living on $150,000 a year now, you may assume that you need 80% of that to retire, which means saving enough to have $120,000 a year in cash flow. But, because of your mortgage, taxes and all the rest, you're not living on $150,000 today but more like $90,000. And, when you figure out what your perfect lifestyle will cost, the amount you need might drop even more. Let's say you want to spend 20 years doing missionary work in South Africa. I figured out that with travel costs, insurance, taxes and basic living costs, you'll need a cash flow of $5,000 a month for 20 years to do that. That's $60,000 a year in cash flow, half of what you assumed. It's possible, more possible than you may think.

Every plan should be projected out to age 100 because life expectancy is increasing and will probably increase more as the Boomers say no to the traditional "retire and rot" concept of their grandparents. If you want to walk away from work at 55, it can be scary to think, "I need to make sure I don't run out of money for 45 years." But it's possible with the right planning and choices on your part. Your team can show you, in impartial math, how it will work.

When Work Becomes Optional

What I love about what I do, especially when I'm able to help people quit obligatory work years early, is that I'm freeing them from worry and regret and turning them loose on the world at the height of their wealth, knowledge and experience. It's liberating to people when they know they may have 40 more years of life ahead of them, and they have no financial worries and no obligations but the ones they choose. Perhaps for the first time, they are free from worry about the future and regret about the past.

It's amazing to see them blossom. They open up businesses. They write novels. They become activists. What a Life and Legacy Plan does is release people from the presumed obligation that they have to either work or not work; it frees people to *work according to their own rules and values.*

This is the difference between survival and prosperity. Prosperity is when you have more than you need. Billions of people spend most of their lives just trying to survive. But when you have a plan, and you update the plan regularly with the help of a trained professional, you can be free from worry and regret, and you can live prosperously.

Now, let's be honest. Some people can't leave work early. Either they didn't save enough, or what is Truly Important to them is too expensive for them to quit working before age 65. However, what my team has also been able to do for quite a few folks is show them that they can quit the high-stress, high-paying jobs they have now and take an "affinity job," that doesn't pay as much but lets them do something they love. I've had clients go to work for The Home Depot, run golf shops and even become river rafting guides. They are the happy people! They know they're still on track toward their ultimate goal, but in the meantime, their stress is nearly 100% gone, and they're enjoying going to work.

This is what some financial advisors call "values-based planning." Most traditional financial planning was based on what was done in the last 100 years, but in the last 10 years, everything has changed. In the past, the presumption was that a person would work until around age 65, retire and stop working completely, and be dead before 80. But the Baby Boom generation has turned that upside down. Now we have to assume that many people, after leaving an obligatory working life behind them, will want to lead active, ambitious, creative lifestyles, that they may well go back to work at something they enjoy or start businesses (meaning additional income), and they will live well beyond 80. The old models no longer make any sense.

Today, you need to be asking three key questions as you head into the Life and Legacy Plan process:

1. What is Truly Important to me? If there was any silver lining to COVID-19, it was the opportunity for many of us to think about how we have been living our lives. Many people are starting to value their lives more. If they have been experiencing abuse and neglect, they are looking to figure out a plan to leave that behind and spend the rest of their time on earth doing what is Truly Important to them with the people who matter most to them.

2. What is my definition of success? This is crucial because I think there's a lot of social pressure to be seen as a "success" after you retire. But is your definition of success driven by someone else's idea? Does it mean you have to own a 100-foot boat and cruise the French Riviera? Or does it mean you're happier and more fulfilled than you have ever been, even if for you that means staying home, planting an incredible garden and starting a little home business selling your handmade preserves? Think about what success means to you.

3. What does my ideal post-work life look like? I want you to draw a picture of your lifestyle after you're no longer working out of need. Where will you be living? Will you travel and where? Will you work? If so, what will you do? What causes will you want to support?

When you have the honest, heartfelt answers to those questions, you're ready for a Life and Legacy Plan.

Your Legacy

We've been focused solely on the Life Plan to this point, but that doesn't make the Legacy Plan any less important. Unfortunately, many people don't like to talk about their legacy because it implies that they're going to die, and that's something most would rather not think about. But we're all going to go someday, so why not face up to it and make the best of it? You do that with a Legacy Plan, something that extends your values and caring beyond your lifespan, making you the next best thing to immortal.

Part of the Legacy Plan means having the legal documents in place to leave a financial legacy for your children and grandchildren, and because of that complex legal landscape, it's essential that you engage a team of people who do this for a living. That usually means establishing a relationship with a good estate planning attorney at some point.

But that's just the basic legal and financial skeleton of a Legacy Plan. It's only about your *extrinsic* wealth, and it can be more than that. It can be a way of contributing your *intrinsic* wealth as well.

Earlier, I mentioned the importance of family foundations in passing on your values to your family and involving them in perpetuating those values. That's one way to make your passions part of your legacy, but not the only way. I've also had clients shoot a video of themselves talking to their children and grandkids about who they are and what they care about. The video is kept secret and safe until after both people pass away, and then we share it with their heirs. It's part of their inheritance and a wonderful way to tell young grandchildren or great-grandchildren, "This is who Grandma and Grandpa were."

Your Legacy Plan also comes down to your values. What is most important to you to support or further after you're gone? I've had clients tell me, "Our idea of a perfect retirement is to bounce the check to the undertaker." In other words, they want to spend every cent, which is fine if that's what matters most to them. Others want to leave a certain amount to their heirs, and I always make sure to tell them, "You have the opportunity to impact your great, great, great grandchildren with the decisions you make here today. How would you like to shape the evolution of your family for generations to come?" I can tell you that makes them stop and think for a while. They realize that their legacy decisions have real power.

Exercise: Write Your Eulogy

A life coach once assigned me the exercise of writing my own eulogy—not of the man that I believed I was at the time, but of the man that I aspired to be. Here is my eulogy:

Rob's Eulogy

He loved with all of his heart. He lived with all of his might. He died with honor and no regrets. To mourn the death of this man would be an insult to the life that he lived. Instead, all of us who were touched by this passionate man agree to do as he has asked. We will celebrate his life by truly living ours in this precious moment until we meet again, rejoicing in the knowledge that our dear friend who loved us so fiercely absolutely did not go quietly into the night.

Now, write your own. Download this form at www.Lifeonomics.com.

My Eulogy

Facing the Facts

All of this—the L steps, the Life Team, the Life and Legacy Plan—are all parts of a big picture that enables you to live without worry and regret. When you have all these pieces in place, I believe you have as much control as you can over life and the future. You know the people you care about will be cared for when you're gone and while you're here. You know what you have to earn and how long you have to work. You know you have skilled, trained professionals working for you behind the scenes, making sure your train stays on the tracks. That allows you to live—really live.

I live this way, and the freedom is incredible. I know how much money I need to make this year to stick to my plan for the long term and do what is Truly Important to me by a certain deadline. Any money beyond that I can use to bike ride across Nebraska or give to someone who needs it more than I do. That is the freedom to live as your passion guides you because you're not stuck in the past, torturing yourself for decisions that are done and gone, or biting your nails about a future for which you haven't planned.

It can be challenging to get people to make a Life and Legacy Plan, however. The simplest reason is this: people don't plan because they're afraid to hear what they assume is going to be bad news. They would rather live in ignorance and keep saying, "We'll get to it someday," than get past their apprehension and deal with the facts. There are two fallacies to this thinking. First of all, as we discussed several chapters ago, things are rarely as bad as our anxiety makes them out to be. Usually, the picture is not that bleak.

Second, not knowing doesn't make the bad news go away. Not doing a Life and Legacy Plan because you're afraid of finding out that you won't be able to stop working until you're 70 is like not going to the doctor for a physical because you'll find out you have diabetes. Not knowing doesn't solve anything! All it does is delay you from taking corrective action until your diabetes gets so bad that you go blind or lose a leg. Or, in terms of your finances later in life, until you wind up having to live with your adult children because you can't afford to live on your meager savings. Denial is the child of worry and regret, and it paralyzes your ability to act in your best interest.

The noted author Eckhart Tolle said, "Facing the facts is one of the most empowering things a person can do." That's because once the facts are known, you can take specific steps to solve the problem or at least reduce the damage. Once a problem is known, it is diminished. So, if you have been delaying talking to a wealth advisor or estate planning attorney about a Life and Legacy Plan because you're afraid to find out where you are financially, just breathe. Remember that it's probably not as bad as you think. It might even be great news, but you won't know until you talk to a professional who practices values-based planning and until you find out for yourself what is Truly Important to you. When you learn the facts, I think you'll find yourself pleasantly surprised, relieved and even thrilled at the possibilities that lie before you.

We're almost at the end of our time together. I hope you've enjoyed the journey as much as I have. But please indulge me while I share a few personal stories and some wisdom I hope will help you make smart choices tomorrow in the remaining pages.

Summary

- Money is a tool that you use to accomplish your goals.
- Planning should start with your vision of what your post-work lifestyle should look like, then work backward to cost.
- Facing facts equals freedom.
- A Life Plan covers you from cradle to grave.
- A Legacy Plan ensures you can positively influence the world after you're gone.

- The key day for retirement is the one when you know that you will be able to spend the time you have left on this earth doing only what is Truly Important to you with people who are Truly Important to you.
- Everything depends on cash flow.

To-Do List

- Examine any elements of a Life Plan you have in place.
- Imagine what your ideal legacy would be.
- Envision your perfect retirement lifestyle.
- Talk to your financial advisor about your retirement status.

AFTERWORD

"Life is what happens to you while you're busy making other plans."

—John Lennon

When I was 12 years old, I read a book that changed my life. Actually, it contained one of two quotes that changed my life. The book was *See You At the Top* by Zig Ziglar. In this classic book, Ziglar coined many phrases and ideas that have become self-improvement classics—"Checkup from the neck up," "Hardening of the attitudes," and so on—that it's almost a self-help version of the canon of William Shakespeare. But one sentence in the book set me on the course that's led me here, to you, on this day. It was, "You can get anything you want in this world if you can just help enough other people get what they want."

That was extraordinary to me and so simple as to be ingenious. I think it's a truism of life that the most powerful gift you can give a person is a change in their perspective. Everyone has a different perspective on the world, and it's impossible not to judge someone else's perspective unless you can see things from their point of view, which you can't do unless you've shared the experiences that shaped that perspective. This is the reason for our #1 rule: Let It Be.

Our perspectives tend to be set in stone early and to be based on a superficial understanding of the world and human behavior. We tend to think, especially when we're younger, that things are very black and white: People always do what's in their best interest, their motivations are cut and dried, and to get what we want, we have to out-compete the other guy. It's life as a war, with the winners as survivors. But now and then, an idea comes along that's so profound and makes so much sense that it sparks an "Aha!" moment. That's what Ziglar's quote was for me. After I read it, it was so clear to me that the way I would gain the things and freedom that I wanted was to help others get the same for themselves. *Lifeonomics* is a manifestation of that purpose: to inspire and empower people (including myself) to overcome adversity, live powerfully and love unconditionally, free from worry and regret. I know what people want: peace and prosperity. They want personal peace, which I define as freedom from conflict in their lives and a sense of control, that all things are in order. For some people, peace means having a beautiful home and garden that is a physical representation of the peaceful mental state they want to carry around; for others, it's about being able to travel and enjoy a series of memorable moments secure in the knowledge that they are as prepared as they can be for whatever comes along.

Confidence is having all your ducks in a row.

Prosperity is simpler: having the financial resources to do what is Truly Important to you with the people who are Truly Important to you. It's not a number. It's a lifestyle. That goes back to the Zig Ziglar quote: "If I help enough people find the peace and prosperity they seek, then they will help me achieve it for myself and the people who are Truly Important to me.'

How much pain they have cost us, the evils which have never happened.

—*Thomas Jefferson*

The Definition of Insanity

The second life-changing quote was, "The definition of insanity is doing the same things over and over and expecting a different result." One of our team's goals in creating *Lifeonomics* is to help people overcome the insanity of doing the same things over and over in their life planning—that is, not doing any planning at all. But I'm not a patient man; I don't want to wait 100 years for the slow process of human evolution to bring millions around to the idea of the L Steps and Life and Legacy Planning. I'm passionate about the idea of the "tipping point," as brilliantly laid out by Malcolm Gladwell in his book by the same name. I think that human development often doesn't happen slowly over long periods but with sudden, volcanic changes in perspective. Something happens, then everything changes.

That's what we hope to bring about with *Lifeonomics*—a sudden shift in perspective that empowers people to live in alignment with their purpose, whatever it might be. What happens when people are empowered to live in alignment with their purpose? I've seen it, and I'll tell you: It's an increase in joy and contentment, an end to regret, the loss of the fear of death, revived relationships and a de-emphasis on material acquisition. People stop worrying about *having* and start focusing their energies more on *creating* and *helping*, bringing light and blessings to others who, hopefully, will undergo their own shifts in perspective. Multiply that by a few hundred million, and bingo! You've got a completely new world.

The single most important question for anyone interested in helping people make choices that will dramatically enhance the quality of their lives—coaches, self-help authors, physicians, therapists—is: "How can I get people to make changes that are in their own best interest?" There's a multi-billion-dollar self-improvement industry based on selling a thousand different answers to that question, and it's often a waste of time. The answers are all based on conventional wisdom, and neither I, nor the rest of my team, have much tolerance for that. We prefer *unconventional wisdom*. Rather than talk to someone and lecture them on all the good this choice or that choice will do them, we take a much simpler solution: show them what's possible.

Put Me In, Coach

That's what I do in my other profession as a life coach. I combine my work as a wealth advisor and life coach because, in the end, the values and life choices that I help people discover as a coach are what guide us to their ideal financial solutions for the present and the future. Sound life choices and sound financial choices are inseparable, two sides of the same coin. *Lifeonomics* is as much a coaching and self-improvement program as it is about Life and Legacy Plans. That should be obvious; we've spent most of our time talking about mental disciplines that free us from worry and regret, not about 401(k) accounts. *Lifeonomics* is really about training yourself to let go of worry and regret so that you can make changes that will enhance your life on every front, from health and wealth to purpose and relationships.

So, if you don't believe that people can change, I have one thing to say: Come to one of our offices and let our team of gifted, unconventionally wise people show you. We'll paint some before-and-after pictures that might just blow your mind. Lives change every day if the motivation is strong enough. I have seen people make changes so profound that even they couldn't believe what they had done, guided by the *Lifeonomics* coaching methodology:

1. Figure out what is Truly Important to you in life, your purpose.
2. Teach your mind to let go of worry and regret so you can focus your energies on re-inventing yourself around your purpose.
3. Set goals and have someone to hold you accountable.

4. Create a Life and Legacy Plan.

5. Reach your goals and set new ones.

6. Rinse & Repeat.

> *"Every evening, I turn my worries over to God.*
> *He's going to be up all night anyway."*
>
> —*Mary C. Crowley, founder of Home Interiors & Gifts, Inc.*

Our goal is that **Lifeonomics** as a system can be adopted and used by personal coaches on the intrinsic wealth side and by financial advisors on the financial side and that, by adopting this philosophy, we will have an exponential impact on the human race. We want to create an even larger community of like-minded people who will get **Lifeonomics** out there and bring about more of the kinds of change we see in my office every day. As Margaret Mead said, "Never doubt that a small group of thoughtful people can change the world. Indeed, it's the only thing that ever has."

Coach, Advise, Teach and Inspire

What we're trying to do in our wealth management practice and our coaching is to help people reach *self-actualization*, the pinnacle of Dr. Abraham Maslow's hierarchy, the peak of personal development, where the person is the best he or she can be. Not many people think in terms of making themselves the best they can be; instead, they spend most of their time worrying about survival and finding excuses why they can't change things. But what if you could get past that? What if you could let go of worry and regret and use your energy to be the absolute best you can be? And if you're not thinking in those terms, why not?

I don't need to contribute to global change to be happy with my life; I could die tomorrow with no regrets at all. But my purpose is to help others reach self-actualization, free of worry and regret, and turn themselves loose to do what is Truly Important to them with the people they cherish. I hope that this book has helped to light the way to personal transformation for you and that it's made you think and challenge some of your preconceptions. I hope you'll be one of the many readers who will go to www.Lifeonomics.com to find out about coaching and self-transformation. Speaking for my team and the **Lifeonomics** community, it would be an honor to be part of the next, most exciting stage of your story.

So, I'll leave you with a statement of purpose, the one that guides my wealth management practice, my team, my coaching and my life:

*"To coach and advise some, to teach and inspire many,
to have love and compassion for all."*

APPENDIX I:

Now that you've read ***Lifeonomics***, you've put yourself on the path toward building a financial future that reflects what really matters to you. This is a whole new way of looking at your finances and one that is different from what you may have learned from reading other books on financial planning, listening to podcasts on money, or working with traditionally trained financial advisors. While it's important to build a portfolio that is balanced and reflects your risk tolerance, more essential is planning your life in a way that allows you to direct most of your attention to what is Truly Important to you.

If you embrace the ideas you have learned here, you will find that you will naturally gravitate toward better habits when it comes to managing your finances. Our financial lives don't exist in a vacuum. When you become more mindful in general, you'll become more mindful about your money, too.

Once you are truly operating with mindfulness in your daily life, you'll find you are staying on top of planning more, keeping a better handle on how you're spending, making fewer impulse purchases you regret later and less burdened by debt. Your financial life will come into balance organically, without you having to pore over 10 more books about personal finance. You'll have all of the tools you need.

Like anything worth doing, building a more mindful financial life requires commitment. It's not going to happen without you thinking about it, making space in your life for it, and acting on the principles you've learned here.

But how do you put these ideas into action on a day-to-day basis once you've done the exercises in the chapters? To help you stay on track, here are exercises you can do anytime you need to reconnect with why you picked up this book in the first place and what you learned. You can do these in connection with our Mind, Body and Spirit Challenge, which you can learn about on our website or your own.

Exercise #1: Pay Attention to Your Attention

Let me ask you a question. What are you paying attention to throughout your day? Because what we feed GROWS. And what we starve fades away. We feed the experience of our lives first through our attention.

We see some whose attention is constantly moving, ricocheting from subject to subject. Others' attention is captured by someone or something else, like a cell phone or social media. In other words, their attention is being hacked.

Truly successful people have developed the skill of focused attention, which is a deliberate act of directed free will, holding their attention only on that which is Truly Important to them and the people who are Truly Important to them. This week, I want you to try something. I want you to pay attention... to your attention. Here is an exercise to help you do that.

1. This week, break out your calendar, and for every hour of the day that you are awake, mark the calendar with how you spent the time.

2. At the end of the week, print out the calendar. Highlight the hours you spent giving your focused attention to something, whether it was work, dinner with your family, your workout, or something else.

3. In another color, highlight the times when you were multitasking in some way.

4. Ask yourself how much of the week you gave your focused attention to that which is Truly Important to you and the people who truly matter in your life.

5. If there is room for improvement, use your calendar for next week to schedule more time to give your attention to the things that truly matter to you.

Exercise #2: Breaking Free of Worry and Regret

May I ask a question? What would you do differently in your life if you weren't worried that you would regret the decision?

So far, we have learned to Forget Regret, to Let It Be, Learn From It and Let It Go so we can Live Now, but for many of us, regret is not our primary distraction. What holds us back from truly living our lives in this age of pandemics and turmoil… is worry.

Abraham Hicks once said that worry is using our imagination to create what we *don't* want. The New Testament tells us not to worry about tomorrow, for tomorrow will worry about itself. That each day has trouble enough of its own.

Researchers estimate that we have more than 70,000 thoughts per day. How do you spend yours? Are you worrying about things over which you have no control?

We've also learned that what we feed grows, and what we starve recedes. That we feed the experience of our lives first through our time and attention.

There's an old saying, "Worry is like a rocking chair--it gives you something to do but it doesn't get you anywhere."

We believe worry is a form of self-delusion that makes us feel like we're actively addressing a possible future problem when, in fact, we're doing nothing at all but… thinking… maybe even talking or texting about it… but not doing anything about it.

So, how can we actively address a problem that doesn't exist yet… in a future that doesn't exist yet… that may never really exist at all? We address it with a powerful LIFEtool called… a plan! We can't control life, but we can plan for it!

This week's challenge is to make a thorough worry list. Rank each worry from 1-10, with 10 being the biggest. Then, ask a question about each: Do I really have any control over this? If the answer is no.

Let it go. If the answer is yes, it's time to plan!

Exercise #3: Restore your focus

The year was 1988. I was spending my Saturday morning at a friend's house watching cartoons with their four-year-old boy, Chase. Chase loooooved cartoons and he loooooved to talk about them with me. That morning, he was in my lap, nose to nose, telling me a Truly Important story about the cartoon we had just watched when his mother walked into the room and asked me a question. After I talked to her for about a minute, Chase had his fill. He gently reached out and, with his little hands, grabbed both of my ears and slowly turned my head back around until we were nose to nose once again.

Chase was simply not interested in my time without my attention. To him, my conversation with his mother was just a distraction.

Fast forward 30 years. Technology has permeated our lives, offering unprecedented distractions unimaginable back in 1988. Big tech companies and plenty of others are making trillions of dollars every year by hacking our attention. In fact, we're hacking your attention right now to help you restore focus on what's Truly Important to you.

Let me ask you a question: Is someone important in your life trying to grab your ears? Probably! To restore focus on the people and things that are Truly Important to you, it's important to "grab your own ears."

Here's an exercise to help you do that.

1. List the people in your life who have been trying to "grab your ears" the past month.
2. List the people whose ear-grabbing has motivated you to give them your full attention.

3. Ask yourself if the people who've gotten your full attention are the ones who are Truly Important to you.

4. If you've been giving your attention to people who are not Truly Important to you, how can you avoid letting that happen in the future? You may not be able to avoid certain work-related meetings and calls, but is there a way you can reduce how much they cut into your personal time?

5. If you have not been giving your attention to people who are Truly Important to you, how can you address that gap in the coming week? Is it possible to schedule one-on-one time in your calendar with your spouse, children, or friends? What gets scheduled gets done.

Exercise #4: Deciding Is Suffering

Do you suffer from decision fatigue? One simple definition of a plan is a series of decisions made in advance on how we will respond to a future moment. Systems, Strategies and Structures are all forms of planning.

So, why is planning so important when living in the moment is the ultimate goal? The first reason is something called decision fatigue. A key foundational concept for our LIFEcoaching methodology is that Deciding is Suffering. It's estimated that we make over 35,000 decisions each day! That's a lot of suffering! It results in something called decision fatigue. Turns out, one of the most powerful ways to increase energy and reduce overall fatigue is to reduce the number of decisions that we make in a day.

Another reason why planning is so important is that with each decision we make, we increase the probability of choosing unwisely, especially if the decision is made… you guessed it… when we're fatigued. What happens then? Things like matching tattoos on a first date and mullet haircuts!

The last reason that planning is so important is the most important one. If we truly believe in our planning process, if we truly believe in our

Systems, Strategies and Structures… it absolutely DOES free us to live in the moment and let go of worry in a chaotic world.

We learn from the past and plan for the future so we can live powerfully in the present moment. This week's challenge is to simply focus on how many decisions you are making each day and to look for ways to reduce that number so that you can focus more on doing only that which is Truly Important with the people who are Truly Important to us in the only moment that matters… right now!

Exercise #5: Cradle to the Grave

Life is an amazing gift. One of the simplest descriptions of a person's life is the distance between the cradle and the grave. This distance is measured by time, days, weeks, months, years, decades.

Now, we never know exactly where we are on that line. When I was about three years old, my older brother Nathan was killed in a tragic accident. The distance between his cradle and grave was only eight years.

So, how do we make the most of the time/life we have left, understanding that the only time we really have is now? Remember the line from *Spaceballs*, "When will *then* be *now?*" Answer… Soon!

What if we could spend the rest of the time we have left on this earth focused on only doing that which is Truly Important to us… With the people who are Truly Important to us? In today's world, almost everything else can be automated, delegated, or eliminated.

Write this question down on a bunch of sticky notes and place them everywhere in your life… on your computer screen, on your mirror, beside your bed: *Is what I'm doing right now Truly Important to me?*

Keep a small notebook at your side this week. Each time you find yourself staring at one of those sticky notes, write down what you are doing (working, washing the car, talking with your mom on the phone, whatever) and make a checkmark after those activities that are Truly Important to you.

Exercise #6: Restoring Honor

In our life coaching methodology, we define honor as doing what we say we'll do and being who we say we are.

Flashback to 1988. I knew a very ambitious 24-year-old financial advisor. He was single, had just moved to the big city, and was getting started with his career. He wanted to be successful, so he hired a life coach.

His first assignment was to write down three to five things that were "most important" to him. His list was simple and noble: Faith, Family, and Career. His second assignment was to document in his paper Day-Timer calendar (because that's all we had back then) every 30 minutes of his life for one full week without changing anything.

The next week, the young man turned in his assignment. To his horror, the life coach pulled out a calculator and proceeded to add up all of his hours that week to see how he was spending his time and attention. He came to find out there was almost zero time spent forwarding his faith. He didn't call home or see any of his family. Although he was "at work" based on the activities listed, he was only actually working about 20 hours that week trying to grow his career.

The life coach handed him back the real list of what was most important to him. They were: Drinking beer, watching cable TV and dating girls (or attempting to date girls). The reason I know this story so well is because I was that young financial advisor.

Now, we certainly don't think there's anything inherently wrong with drinking beer, watching cable TV and dating girls. It's the misalignment that was the problem. I was unintentionally living a life that was completely out of integrity. I was not doing what I said I would do, nor was I being who I said I was. I was living without honor.

Now that you've realigned your time and attention, you may realize that there are areas of your life that are out of integrity with who you say you are. There are relationships that may have had your time but not much of your attention, and there may be things you have said you would do that have not yet been done.

This week's challenge is a big one: Focus on restoring honor and integrity in all things, large and small, with all people, friends, and foes.

1. Make a list of three or more activities that you have said you would do but have not done yet, or some of the relationships you care about deeply but don't give your time to.
2. For each of these items, list a first step you can take in the next month to reallocate your time so that the items on your list get some necessary attention.
3. Put the first step for each on your calendar at a specific time.
4. Mark a date on your calendar where you will take stock of how you did on taking these first steps. If you have not taken the first steps, ask yourself why. Is it possible that what you think is important to you is not? Is there an obstacle standing in your way, like an unpredictable work schedule, that you need to plan around?
5. For the items you consider Truly Important, repeat steps 2, 3, and 4 for the following month. If you have not taken any action toward prioritizing something or someone that is Truly Important to you, consider removing them from the list.

For the things you do spend your time on, notice the exponential power that can show up when you start restoring honor to your activities. Write down how it feels to know you made good on your commitments to yourself.

Exercise #7: The "Triple C" Challenge

"Don't criticize, condemn, or complain" is Principle Number One in Dale Carnegie's landmark book *How to Win Friends and Influence People.* Applying it will recapture amazing amounts of time and energy that can be re-directed toward doing that which is Truly Important to you with the people who are Truly Important to you.

Here's the Mind, Body, and Spirit Triple "C" Challenge: Don't criticize, condemn, or complain for seven days (especially not in writing in a text or on social media)—even if you think they deserve it.

Here are our definitions of each:

Criticize: Make unsolicited negative comments, especially in the absence of a viable solution or to someone who cannot control it.

Criticizing someone behind their back is gossip. Gossip is TOXIC! Momma used to say, "Son, if you don't have something nice to say about someone, try saying nothing at all." It's simple advice that works.

Condemn: Also called judging, condemning is deeming someone or something "wrong," especially without knowing all the facts. The act of condemning allows you to get a quick fix of unearned superiority. Though this has become our new national cybersport, it is very destructive to you and those around you.

Complain: Sharing negative news or opinions, especially with someone who cannot effect change, won't serve you well. Telling your waiter that your food is cold is a legitimate concern shared with someone who can correct the problem. Repeatedly telling a friend that your spouse just isn't "doing it for you" anymore is complaining! Stop complaining and get some counseling.

The Triple Cs, particularly when you do them all at once, steal massive amounts of our time and attention while often creating even more massive relationship problems with others and the world.

What would happen if, for the next seven days, you suddenly redirected any Triple C energy you're putting forth toward doing something constructive?

Try doing it for a week and then write down your observations in a notebook you can look back at if you are tempted to indulge in the Triple C's.

Exercise #8: Be Impeccable with Your Word

In his landmark book *The Four Agreements*, one of the agreements author Don Miguel Ruiz shares is to be impeccable with your word. "The human mind is like a fertile ground where seeds are continually being planted," says Ruiz. "By hooking our attention, the word can enter our mind and change a whole belief for better or for worse."

My late mother was someone ALL of my friends growing up called Mom. Everyone, I mean everyone, who's ever met my momma loved her. She would never intentionally hurt anyone, especially not one of her boys, but the power of the spoken word is immense. She had no idea what she was doing the day I chose one of my greatest insecurities in life. You see, my momma was only five foot two inches tall, and for most of her adult life, she weighed over two hundred pounds. It was a personal demon that she had never been able to slay. In fact, she blamed her weight most of all when her marriage to my dad fell apart and ended in divorce after 31 years together. The closest thing to a curse word that I ever heard come out of her mouth was directed at herself... yeah... the "F" word (fat).

My lifelong insecurity was born from a simple, innocent and loving remark that she would often make to me growing up. "Robby, I'm so sorry. Your skinny little brother took after your daddy, but it looks like you're going to take after me."

I believed her. The seed took root in the fertile ground of my young mind, and I have struggled with my weight on and off for most of my life. No matter how many thousands of miles I ride my bike each year, part of me will always see myself as that chubby kid getting bullied on the playground. And I'm a LIFE coach! That's how powerful words can be.

This week's challenge is to live the first agreement: "Be impeccable with your word. Speak with integrity. Say only what you mean. Avoid using the word to speak against yourself or gossip about others. Use the power of your word in the direction of truth and love.

Exercise #9: Face the Facts/Resist the Fix

Many of us go through our entire lives "reacting" to our world and others in one of three ways:

- *Denial:* This is the opposite of grabbing our ears. It's the act of sticking our fingers in our ears, shutting our eyes, and going "Lalala Lalala." It's the decision to ignore something that may be very important.
- *Delusion:* Delusion is the act of believing something that is just not factually accurate. My friend, who passed away, deluded herself into believing that the lower back pain was just a kidney infection without getting the proper tests.
- *Fixing:* The instant need to categorize everything as good or bad, right or wrong, when we don't have all of the facts is what I call "fixing." It is our mind's way to take shortcuts and force everything we observe to fit into our worldview.

Fixing is also an attempt to control that which we have no control over. Life can be lived. It cannot be controlled.

A powerful process we call the "L Steps" can give us the tools to break these old habits that are robbing us of our time, attention, energy, and enjoyment.

The L Step process is as follows:

Let It Be + Learn From It + Let It Go = Live Now

The first L Step is to Let It Be. Let It Be is an incredibly powerful LIFEtool that can change the quality of our lives almost immediately. Let It Be starts with the act of acceptance and ultimately leads to something we call compassionate detachment.

Accepting something does NOT mean we have to like it or approve of it. For instance, bad things sometimes happen to good people. This is a fact. Living in denial or delusion regarding this fact only causes unnecessary suffering in the world. Trying to "fix" this fact by saying something like "Maybe they really weren't good people" doesn't help, either.

Many years ago, I was vacationing with my family at a lodge on top of a mountain. As you'll recall from Chapter Five, my then-10-year-old stepson Kevin, jumped onto a ledge well off the beaten track when he was playing and landed right on a poisonous snake. Kevin screamed. The snake bit him several times in self-defense.

This resulted in an airlift by helicopter and about a week's stay at our local Children's Hospital. Though Kevin recovered completely, it would have been easy for all of us to judge the snake as bad or wrong, or ask the universe WHY this innocent child had to suffer, but instead, we chose to Let It Be. The snake was just doing what snakes do. Kevin was just doing what 10-year-old boys do. That's the end of it. Lesson learned.

This week's challenge is to Let It Be: Face the facts. Resist the fix. When someone does something that upsets you… Let It Be. When your hair dryer blows up in the middle of getting ready for a big meeting… Let It Be. It's just a hairdryer. Sometimes they blow up. It's probably not the universe telling you not to go to the meeting. When something terrible happens in the world and you see it on the news, Let It Be what it is… A tragedy. Resist the fix of judging the people involved without knowing all the facts. Take sticky notes, write Let It Be on them and stick them all over your house and workspace. In all things great or small, the first step toward true personal freedom is to Let It Be.

Exercise #10: Learn From It

"Learn From It" does not simply mean to increase your knowledge of something. It means getting ready for change. Simply educating someone does not guarantee change. Ask any teacher.

When I was a teenager out on the farm, a stray dog wandered up and joined our other dogs. We called her Chance. Chance was a good dog, but she had some issues. One of them was the tractor. She hated it and would bark incessantly at Dad while he was trying to work. One day, she finally got so mad she bit the tractor wheel and held on. Before Dad could stop, he had rolled over her head. Fortunately, the ground was soft where he was working, so it did no permanent damage to her, but man, did it get her attention! She never barked at tractors ever again! Momma said, "Looks like Chance really learned her lesson." That's how "Learn From It" was born, because Chance didn't want to blow her second Chance!

After we Let It Be and face the facts of a situation without judgment or attachment, the next step is to Learn From It to change. Now, I may be about to step on a lotta people's toes here, but I believe we can only truly change that which we have control over, and we only have control over three things:

1. Our own thoughts.
2. Our own words.
3. Our own actions.

We may have some effect, maybe even some influence, on other things or people, but we most certainly have no control. The LIFEtool that we use to help exercise control over our Thoughts, Words and Actions we call The 3 S's (and, yes, we like ideas that start with the same letter because they are easier to remember)

The 3 S's are:

1. **Systems:** These can be simple. When I was younger, I used to have a problem keeping up with my car keys. It would sometimes cause

me to be late for work, and I lost time and energy looking for them, but most of all, it made me feel stupid. Instead of continuing the delusion that someday I was going to wake up and suddenly be the kind of guy who never lost his keys, I solved the problem with a simple system. It's a key fob hanging on my belt. This key fob can only live in two places: on my belt loop or on the wall in my bedroom. Problem solved.

2. **Strategies**: This is defined as a plan of action. The difference between a system and a strategy is that we may only need to use a strategy when faced with certain circumstances and not in everyday life. We may have a strategy for surviving a bear attack, but we hope we'll never need to use it!

3. **Structure:** Structure is a fixed set of accountabilities. It reduces the number of decision points in our lives. My team fills my day with meetings and appointments. This creates Structure for me. Without it… Well, let's just say I don't get as much done.

Take inventory of all of the Systems, Strategies and Structures that you already have deployed in your life. Where do you need new ones?

Exercise #11: Let It Go

When I was a teenager, my dad tried to teach me to drive in his prized 1972 Chevy pickup, which he loved almost as much as me. He noticed I was having a hard time keeping the truck in the lane. I kept veering toward the shoulder.

"Son, where are you looking?" he asked me.

"I'm looking at the front corner of the truck and trying not to cross the white line," I replied.

"Son, try this," he said. "Stop focusing on the rumble strip and trying not to hit it. Instead, shift your focus much farther down the road and drive to that point. Drive to the place you want to be." Problem solved. I never swerved again!

We will drive TO whatever we focus ON.

In the United States of America, we have a right called double jeopardy that prohibits multiple prosecutions for the same offense, yet many of us don't allow ourselves that right at all. We make a choice we perceive as a mistake and then punish ourselves for it over and over and over. We have bought into the myth that "good people" have lots of guilt and regret about the choices and/or mistakes they have made in their lives. That's how we know they're good people! It seems silly to continue punishing ourselves for choices or mistakes by finishing the entire trip riding on the rumble strip, but that's what happens! We obsess or revisit mistakes far past the point of usefulness. We live in a world of regret, obsessing over a past we cannot change.

In our life coaching methodology, we believe life is supposed to be catch and release, not catch and carry. We believe guilt is supposed to be the rumble strip on life's highway, not a lane! We get a little course, the rumble strip makes a big noise, and we quickly self-correct to get back on course.

If you're caught up in guilt and regret, it's possible to break free. Make a list of every single regret you have. Care enough about yourself to be brutally honest. Write them all down on a piece of paper. Then apply the L Steps:

1. Let It Be what it is. Face the facts with as little judgment as possible.
2. Then ask yourself, "Did I learn from this?" "Have I changed my Thoughts, Words and Actions… adapted my Systems, Strategies and Structures?"
3. If not, by all means, do so. If you have Learned From It…
4. LET IT GO… Take my dad's advice, grab your own ears, shift your focus down the road and drive to where you want to be.

Exercise #12: Live Now

One of our favorite definitions of mindfulness includes two main concepts:

1. Self-regulation of attention so it is focused on the present moment. (We like to call this grabbing your own ears)
2. Taking an open, curious, accepting, non-resistant stance toward one's experience. (We call that Take Life as Coaching)

"Realize deeply that the present moment is all you have. Make the NOW the primary focus of your life," Eckhart Tolle writes in his amazing book, *The Power of Now* (which, if it's not on your bookshelf, you should order now). It may or may not actually be all that we have. I'll leave that question up to the spiritual leaders and the quantum physicist. But one thing we know for sure, it is all we have control over (and we know that obsession over that which we have no control is futile).

Although mindfulness has been around for thousands of years, it seems to have fairly recently become a huge part of modern culture. Even my iPhone reminds me to "breathe and be mindful." Seems like everyone agrees that mindfulness is beneficial to achieve. However, few are actually telling us how to do it. That being said, I have really good news!

If you've been participating in our Mind, Body and Spirit challenge, you already have the basic training to achieve mindfulness in a world of distraction! Every lesson and every challenge up until now has already been empowering you with the LIFEtools to live the life you have left completely present and fully engaged! That's the journey we're already on!

This week's challenge has the power to permanently change your life experience. Find someone who loves you and knows you, who already knows about some or all of those regrets you have written down on that list. Go outside and find someplace safe to do this, take the list, and set it on fire. You see, you don't need those regrets anymore.

APPENDIX II:

RECOMMENDED READING

Many books can help you in your journey to building a life around what matters most to you. Here are my favorites.

Atomic Habits: An Easy & Proven Way to Build Good Habits & Break Bad Ones by James Clear

Tiny, incremental changes in our lives can have remarkable results. As James Clear shows in this bestselling classic, an ideal way to do that is by bringing Systems, Strategies and Structures to your life.

Living from a Place of Surrender: The Untethered Soul in Action by Michael Singer

If you're looking to take your spiritual practice to the next level, this audiobook is full of valuable teachings that come directly from Michael Singer. The book is a recording of Singer's first-ever online course.

Peak Mind: Find Your Focus, Own Your Attention, Invest 12 Minutes a Day by Amishi P. Jha

This is a no-fluff, science-based entry-level guide to building focus and attention. As such, it offers a perfect companion to Lifeonomics.

The 5 Resets: Rewire Your Brain and Body for Less Stress and More Resilience by Aditi Nerurkar, M.D.

We've all been told chronic stress is hurting us but how can we reduce its impact? This book, based on medical science, offers a pathway to change, with easily implemented techniques.

The Four Agreements by Don Miguel Ruiz

Everything that happens in life is a result of the agreements we make with ourselves and the world, as Don Miguel Ruiz points out. This book will help you change those agreements and, as a result, how the world treats you and how you treat yourself.

The Road Less Traveled: A New Psychology of Love, Traditional Values and Spiritual Growth by M. Scott Peck, M.D.

M. Scott Peck was the first writer to show how psychology intersected with spirituality in a way that was a huge breakthrough. I love his work and to this day use his definition of love, which is the will to extend oneself for the spiritual growth of oneself or another.

The Untethered Soul: The Journey Beyond Yourself by Michael Singer

Michael Singer is an ideal guide to learning how to live in the present and let go of the thoughts that drain our energy and keep us from living in the moment.

The Power of Now: A Guide to Spiritual Enlightenment by Eckardt Tolle

What we really need to do is live our purpose in the moment. That's when God shows up, and the world changes. Coaching and planning for the future help us get there. This book is accepted by almost all wisdom traditions.

When I Say No, I Feel Guilty by Manuel J. Smith

This assertiveness training bestseller from 1975, which my mother bought but apparently never read, was the first self-help book I ever picked up. I was being bullied at the time. It impacted me in a very powerful way and got me interested in reading other self-help books.

APPENDIX III:

Tap the Power of 12-step Groups

Codependency often develops when we try to protect someone who is an addict from the consequences of their behavior. Breaking the silence in a safe, confidential environment is one of the most powerful tools for healing. Peer groups, where we can meet anonymously with other people who are also coping with a loved one's addiction, are the most direct path to healing.

Here are some groups that can help. Many now have virtual and phone meetings.[6]

Al-Anon (al-anon.org): Families and friends of alcoholics.
Adult Children of Alcoholics (adultchildren.org): Grown children of alcoholics and dysfunctional families.

---

[6] **Please note:** The information being provided is strictly as a courtesy. When you link to any of the websites provided here, you are leaving this book. We make no representation as to the completeness or accuracy of information provided at these websites. Nor is the company liable for any direct or indirect technical or system issues or any consequences arising out of your access to or your use of third-party technologies, websites, information or programs made available through this website. When you access one of these websites, you assume total responsibility and risk for your use of the websites to which you are linking.

Debt-Anon (debtanon.org): Families and friends of compulsive debtors.

Gam-Anon (gam-anon.org): Families and friends of compulsive gamblers.

Nar-Anon (nar-anon.org): Families and friends of narcotics addicts.

S-Anon (sanon.org): Families and friends of sex addicts.

Disclosures

Robert Holdford| CEO & Senior Wealth Advisor

Wealth Management, Inc.

rob@canistillretire.com

10809 Executive Center Drive | Suite 319

Little Rock, AR 72211

Local: 501-217-4069

Fax: 501-217-9775

Toll free: 877-211-4069

www.canistillretire.com

Securities offered through Cetera Wealth Services LLC, member FINRA/ SIPC. Investment advisory services offered through CWM, LLC, an SEC Registered Investment Advisor. Cetera is under separate ownership from any other named entity.

These examples are hypothetical and do not represent actual people or performance of any particular investments. Investments in securities do not offer a fixed rate of return. Principal, yield and/or share price will fluctuate with changes in market conditions and when sold or redeemed, you may receive more or less than originally invested. The opinions contained in this material are those of the author, and not a recommendation or solicitation to buy or sell investment products. This information is from sources believed to be reliable, but Cetera Wealth Services, LLC cannot guarantee or represent that it is accurate or complete. All investing involves risk, including the possible loss of principal. There is no assurance that any investment strategy will be successful.

ACKNOWLEDGEMENTS

While I am the author of this book, there are many people without whom it would never have existed and to whom I owe profound thanks.

At the top of my list are the individuals who chose to share their stories while remaining anonymous, some of whom are no longer with us. Your openness shaped this book more than you may ever know.

I also owe immense gratitude to the Lifeonomics coaching staff, led by Steve Biermann, my brother Joel Holdford and Amy Constable, and as well as my contributing editor, Elaine Pofeldt.

Steve Biermann has been both a collaborator and a true creative partner in developing the content and coaching material you've read about. In doing so, he has been the producer, co-developer, and creative heartbeat of this project. Around here, we call him "Producer Steve," and the title fits.

My brother Joel has also been an essential part of our team. A retired military chief of police and a 100% disabled veteran, he has brought the leadership and integrity he developed during his years of service to our country to our organization and this book. His support, insight, and commitment have been invaluable—especially the hours we've spent together on our weekly calls, where we've developed, refined, and challenged ideas.

Amy, too, has been part of that creative heartbeat. She has read drafts, tested concepts, and kept us honest, challenging us to dig deep during the many months we spent on this project. She has volunteered countless hours of her time to both coaching and developing our entire Lifeonomics methodology for many years now.

Elaine is a brilliant freelance writer, editor, and author of *Tiny Business, Big Money* and *The Million-Dollar, One-Person Business.* Everybody needs a coach, and she has been far more than a contributing editor for this project. There is absolutely no way I would have been able to complete this without her coaching, contributing, and writing expertise. I may be the author, but she's the true writer on the team.

I also want to thank Omani Carson and the team at Carson Group, who have been powerful influences. I would further like to thank the compliance team at Carson Group for their guidance and professionalism.

I would also like to thank my entire Wealth Management, Inc. team—our "Wealth Team," as we call it—for their support and dedication during this project: Janet Carpenter, our Vice-President of Operations of more than 30 years; Crystal Baker, who leads our Client Service; and our Wealth Advisors, Caroline Rodriguez and Ron Lee. Without your work and dedication, I wouldn't have been able to do mine.

Of course, I must mention my biggest fan and the person most personally impacted by Lifeonomics: my amazing wife, Joy Holdford. She's been there through it all, supporting and living the principles we teach. Joy, thank you for your patience, your humor, and for living these principles with me every day.

Special thanks to Jane Tabachnick, my publisher. Although this is a business relationship, it is also a true creative partnership. Thank you to the designers, formatters, and the entire team behind the scenes who brought this book to life with professionalism and care.

Matt Werner has been both a sounding board and a spiritual inspiration throughout this process. His feedback, kindness, and example as a yoga teacher and human being continue to shape how I live and teach. Matt, thank you for being part of our Lifeonomics community and for helping us all breathe a little deeper.

Thanks also to our app developer, Light, whose creativity helps bring Lifeonomics to life in new ways.

I owe a great deal to those who helped keep me physically and mentally balanced during this process: my therapist, Joe Boatright, whose wisdom and perspective have been a weekly anchor, and Dr. Darren Beavers, my chiropractor, who kept me moving through long days at the desk.

This book literally wouldn't have been written without their help.

On a broader level, I want to acknowledge what I call my "Life Team," the people who embody Lifeonomics by showing up, supporting, and living these principles with me every day. My brother Joel and my sister-in-law, Amber Holdford, are part of that inner circle. My extended family, who love, challenge, and ground me, are all part of this as well.

And finally, thanks to everyone who believed in this project: the readers and coaches who are part of the Lifeonomics movement. You remind me daily that this isn't just a book or a business; it's a community built on growth, generosity, and gratitude.

Disclaimer

The views and opinions expressed in this book are solely those of the author and do not necessarily reflect the views of Wealth Management, Inc., Carson Group, Cetera Wealth Services LLC, or any other organization mentioned. This content is for informational and educational purposes only and should not be construed as financial advice or an endorsement by any firm or individual.